T0135935

Proof theory

Compact companion 3

Herman Ruge Jervell
University of Oslo

Bibliographic information published by the Deutsche Nationalbibliothek

The Deutsche Nationalbibliothek lists this publication in the Deutsche Nationalbibliografie; detailed bibliographic data are available in the Internet at http://dnb.d-nb.de.

ISBN 978-3-8325-3303-8

Logos Verlag Berlin GmbH
Comeniushof, Gubener Str. 47,
10243 Berlin
Tel.: +49 (0)30 42 85 10 90
Fax: +49 (0)30 42 85 10 92
INTERNET: http://www.logos-verlag.de

Contents

Preface

Throughout logic there is a tension between the finite and the infinite. Gaisi Takeuti has talked about his conversations between Kurt Gödel and himself. They often used the finite versus the infinite mind as a useful distinction. Our mind is clearly finite, but we have some conceptions about what an infinite mind would be like. In proof theory we take this distinction and this tension seriously. Let us list some places where we use infinite constructions:

Natural numbers: We have as a start the zero and the successor function as a unary constructor.

Data structure: More start objects and more constructors.

Formal language: The language is often given by its signature which tells us the form of the atomic formulas and the construction of compound formulas.

Formal system: We have axioms and rules similar to starts and successors.

Formal process: We have a start of the process and a program which tells us how to get from one configuration in the calculation to the next.

In the development of proof theory we have some classical work done in 1919-45.

Thoralf Skolem: Around 1919 he read Russell and Whiteheads Principia Mathematicae where they developed a new foundation for mathematics. They used much space to prove the simplest arithmetical truths. For Skolem this was not a sign of deep insight. Skolem developed instead three parts simultaneously

Data structure: Natural numbers as a data structure

Programming language: Primitive recursive functions as defining new named operations and relations on the data structure. They are defined by their recursion equations.

Programming logic: Above the programming language Skolem defined a logic. He used ordinary quantifier free logic with use of free variables — and in the calculus he had both the recursion equations from the programming language and induction over quantifier free formulas which may contain free variables.

This was published in 1923.

David Hilbert: Proof theory was introduced as a parallel to number theory. Hilbert hoped that the development of his ϵ-calculus and simple proofs of some theorems in the calculus could effect a reduction of the infinite calculi to the finite realm. Kurt Gödel proved in 1931 that this was not possible — destroying some of Hilberts aims. But his conception of proof theory is very much alive.

Kurt Gödel: In 1931 he proved his incompleteness theorem showing that in formal systems strong enough to treat data structures there will be sentences that are true but not provable. His proof does not involve any analysis of the systems used — the Gödel sentence is constructed in a very general way.

Gerhard Gentzen: In papers 1935-45 he developed proof theory to maturity. Among other things he showed that the Gödel sentence for first order arithmetic could be taken as a sentence expressing transfinite induction up to ε_0. More about this later. Gödel was so impressed by this that he developed his own way of understanding it — following Gentzens lead.

Alan Turing: His analysis of formal processes in 1937 — the turing machines — connected the development of proof theory with theory of computations.

Proof theory is a large subject — too large to be contained in a short book. We have concentrated on some key topics. In particular we have written about ordinal notations. These are objects which are particularly developed within proof theory and are heavily used in the analysis of proofs. With our theory of finite trees we develop ordinal notations in a way which makes the connections to combinatorics clear. The last chapter on finite labeled trees gives our version of Gaisi Takeutis ordinal diagrams. We have proved that they are wellfounded — and from there there are a number of ways to develop the theory, but this is not done here.

We have written this book as a compact companion — any reasonable graduate book in logic should give the background. But it may also be helpful to look at the two previous compact companions.

Direct arguments *1*

1.1 Auxiliary constructions

Skolem had in his 1923 paper three levels:

Universe: Built up from a starting point with one constructor.

Language: Built up from atomic pieces with a number of constructors.

Calculus: Built up from axioms using syntactical rules.

Then Gödel showed in 1931 that these levels are similar, and used this to get the incompleteness. If we now look closer at the levels we see a difference:

Direct construction: The first two levels build up from some simple elements getting more and more complicated pieces.

Constructions via detours: In the last level we may construct something quite simple by having a detour through some quite complicated constructions.

These constructions via detours is what the second incompleteness theorem indicates. There we consider the Gödel sentence

$$\neg \Box \bot$$

which is a short form for the sentence expressing that the falsity $\perp$ is not provable within the system. Gödels second incompleteness says that $\neg\Box\perp$ is not provable — we cannot exclude the possibility that there is a very complicated way of proving $\perp$ using some tricky detours.

Gerhard Gentzen did all the main work towards an understanding of direct constructions in the 1930's. This is — in our view — the way forward from Gödel.

1.2 Sequent calculus

Gentzen introduced sequent calculus. We consider here the following version:

Axioms	$\Gamma, L, \neg L$	$\Gamma, s = s$
Connectives	$\dfrac{\Gamma, F \quad \Gamma, G}{\Gamma, F \wedge G}$	$\dfrac{\Gamma, F, G}{\Gamma, F \vee G}$
Quantifiers	$\dfrac{\Gamma, Fa}{\Gamma, \forall x.Fx}$	$\dfrac{\Gamma, Ft, \exists x.Fx}{\Gamma, \exists x.Fx}$
Equality and cut	$\dfrac{\Gamma, L, L^{\star}, \neg s = t}{\Gamma, L, \neg s = t}$	$\dfrac{\Gamma, F \quad \Delta, \neg F}{\Gamma, \Delta}$
Trivial rule	$\dfrac{\Gamma}{\Gamma}$	

We remind ourselves

- sequents are finite sets of formulas

- the L's in the axioms and the equality rule are literals — atomic formulas or negation of them

- negation $\neg$ is an operation on formulas built up from literals defined in an obvious way

- the a in the $\forall$-rule is a new parameter

- the s and t in the $\exists$-rule and the $=$-rule are terms

- the $L^\star$ in the $=$-rule is obtained from L by substituting some s for t and some t for s

- we develop the theory mostly without $=$ making the exposition simpler. We could as well have included $=$ in the development with just a few changes but leave that to the reader

In the development we have two interpretations of the rules

Analysis: We try to falsify the sequents — propagate upwards, sequents interpreted conjunctively, branching disjunctively

Synthesis: We try to make the sequents valid — propagate downwards, sequents interpreted disjunctively, branching conjunctively

Here is a short summary of the completeness of the rules — as done by Skolem in 1922 and also by Gödel in 1930

We make the analysis fair — everything which could be analyzed is sooner or later analyzed. The analysis is succesful if we have a fair branch not containing an axiom. If the analysis is not succesful, then every branch contains an axiom. We get completeness of sequent calculus by observing that a fair branch not containing an axiom will give a falsification of every formula in the branch. The falsification is given as a quite simple term model.

Gentzen singled out the cut rule as worthy of further study

- The calculus is complete without the cut rule

- The cut rule is used in mathematical practice. The use of lemmas and theorems can be seen as uses of the cut rule.

- Use of the cut rule can dramatically reduce the length of the proof.

- We can eliminate the cut rule at the expense of a super exponential blow up of the length of the proof

- The cut free rules can be used for automatic deduction. From the conclusion we can calculate the premisses.

- The cut rule introduces an extra element of guessing an appropriate cut formula. We cannot calculate that from the conclusion of the rule.

1.3 Cut elimination

There are two important measures for a proof in sequent calculus:

Height: The height of a proof.

Cut rank: The maximum size of a cut formula in the proof

Lemma 1.1 *We have syntactical operations as below which neither increase height nor rank:*

$$
\begin{aligned}
\vdash \Gamma &\Rightarrow \vdash \Gamma, \Delta \\
\vdash \Gamma, F \wedge G &\Rightarrow \vdash \Gamma, F \\
\vdash \Gamma, F \wedge G &\Rightarrow \vdash \Gamma, G \\
\vdash \Gamma, F \vee G &\Rightarrow \vdash \Gamma, F, G \\
\vdash \Gamma, \forall x.Fx &\Rightarrow \Gamma, Ft \\
\vdash \Gamma(a) &\Rightarrow \vdash \Gamma(t)
\end{aligned}
$$

We talk about:

Connected: Look at the rules of sequential calculus. An occurrence of a part of Γ (or for rule $\exists$ of $\Gamma, \exists x.Fx$) in the conclusion is connected to the occurrences of the same part in the premisses.

Thread: Reflexive, symmetric, transitive closure of "connected to". So a proof is built up by many threads. Each thread gives a set of occurrences of the same syntactical piece, and uppermost parts of a thread belongs either to an axiom or to a main formula in one of the rules.

Extra eigen parameter condition: Given a set of terms T and a proof of Γ. We can always assume that the eigen parameters of the proof are not included in T. This is done by renaming the eigen parameters of the proof in an appropriate way. The renaming does not affect the height or the cut rank of the proof.

Now to the syntactical transformations. This is all done by changing all occurrences in a thread. For the different cases we do:

- Assume that none of the eigen parameters in the proof of Γ occurs in Δ. Then add Δ to all sequents in the proof.

- Replace each $F \wedge G$ with F in the thread of $F \wedge G$. Applications of the rule $\wedge$ with main formula $F \wedge G$ will then be transformed to an application of the trivial rule of the one premiss and the other premiss is chopped away. All other applications of rules or axioms are untouched by this transformation. Similar for replacing $F \wedge G$ with G.

- Replace each $F \vee G$ with F, G in the thread of $F \vee G$. Applications of the rule $\vee$ with main formula $F \vee G$ will then be transformed to an application of the trivial rule. All other applications of rules or axioms are untouched by this transformation.

- Assume that none of the eigen parameters in the proof occurs in t. Replace each $\forall x.Fx$ with Ft in the thread of $\forall x.Fx$. Applications of the rule $\forall$ with main formula $\forall x.Fx$ will then be transformed to an application of the trivial rule. All other applications of rules or axioms are untouched by this transformation.

- Assume that none of the eigen parameters in the proof occurs in t. Replace each a with t in the proof.

There is no similar syntactic transformation of $\exists x.Fx$. The best we can do is the following:

Lemma 1.2 (Herbrand) *Assume we have a proof of $\Gamma, \exists x.Fx$ without eigen parameters. Then there are terms $s, t, \ldots, u$ and a syntactical operation which neither increase height nor cut rank with*

$$\vdash \Gamma, \exists x.Fx \Rightarrow \vdash \Gamma, Fs, Ft, \ldots, Fu$$

This is proved as above — note that we must assume that there are no eigen parameters. The problematic case is when we have eigen parameters in the proof. We then have the situation:

$$\cfrac{\cfrac{\Gamma_1, Fs}{\Gamma_1, \exists x.Fx} \qquad \cfrac{\cfrac{\cfrac{\Gamma_3, Fu}{\Gamma_3, \exists x.Fx}}{\vdots} \qquad \Gamma_2, \exists x.Fx, Ft}{\Gamma_2, \exists x.Fx}}{\Gamma, \exists x.Fx}$$

We have problems replacing $\exists x.Fx$ with $Fs, Ft, \ldots, Fu$ without violating the eigen value conditions. The terms $s, t, \ldots, u$ may contain terms which are used as eigen variables.

But we are able to eliminate uses of the cut rule. The key lemma is the following

Lemma 1.3 (Main lemma for cut elimination) *Assume that we have proofs*

$$\vdash \Gamma, H \ \ and \ \vdash \Delta, \neg H$$

with cut rank less than rank of F. Then there is a proof

$$\vdash \Gamma, \Delta$$

with cut rank less than rank of H. For the resulting height we have cases depending on the formula H

Literal: *Sum of heights.*

Connectives: *Maximum of heights $+1$*

Quantifiers: *Sum of heights*

Proof.

Literals: We start with the proof of $\vdash \Gamma, L$. Then first replace each L with Δ. This transformation may replace axioms $\Theta, L, \neg L$ with $\Theta, \Delta, \neg L$ but we have already proofs of $\vdash \Delta, \neg L$.

Connectives: Using the lemma of syntactical transformation we have for $H = F \wedge G$

$$\vdash \Gamma, F \text{ and } \vdash \Gamma, G \text{ and } \vdash \Delta, \neg F, \neg G$$

without increasing height or cut rank. Then by using cuts on F and G we get

$$\vdash \Gamma, \Delta$$

with cut rank less than rank of H and height increased by 2.

Quantifiers: We investigate $H = \exists x.Fx$. By the syntactical transformation we have for any term t

$$\vdash \Delta, \neg Ft$$

without increasing height or cut rank. Now look at the proof of $\Gamma, \exists x.Fx$:

$$\cfrac{\Gamma_1, Fs}{\Gamma_1, \exists x.Fx} \qquad \cfrac{\cfrac{\cfrac{\Gamma_3, Fu}{\Gamma_3, \exists x.Fx}}{\vdots \quad \Gamma_2, \exists x.Fx, Ft}{\Gamma_2, \exists x.Fx}}{\vdots}$$

$$\Gamma, \exists x.Fx$$

We now replace the $\exists x.Fx$ with Δ and inferences of $\exists x.Fx$ with some cuts with cut rank the rank of Ft

$$\cfrac{\Gamma_1, Fs \quad \Delta, \neg Fs}{\Gamma_1, \Delta} \qquad \cfrac{\cfrac{\cfrac{\Gamma_3, Fu \quad \Delta, \neg Fu}{\Gamma_3, \Delta}}{\vdots \quad \cfrac{\Gamma_2, \Delta, Ft \qquad \Delta, \neg Ft}{\Gamma_2, \Delta}}}{\vdots}$$

$$\Gamma, \Delta$$

The cut rank is not increased, but as height we may get the sum of the two heights. ∎

We can measure the cut complexity of a proof by the pair

- the maximal rank of a cut

- the number of cuts of maximal rank

By picking out a topmost cut of maximal rank we can decrease this measure by a proof transformation as long as there are cuts. Furthermore the procedure gives some perspicuous syntactical transformations. To measure the height we introduce

$$
\begin{aligned}
2_0^x &= x \\
2_{n+1}^x &= 2^{(2_n^x)}
\end{aligned}
$$

Then

Theorem 1.4 (Cut elimination) *Assume we have a proof of* Γ *with height* h *and cut rank* r. *Then we can transform the proof into a cut free proof of height*

$$
2_r^h = 2^{2^{\cdot^{\cdot^{\cdot^{2^h}}}}}
$$

It may be useful to sum up why we get the super exponential growth of height when we eliminate cuts:

- the cuts are eliminated systematically by using cuts with smaller cut formulas

- we eliminate cuts of connectives anywhere in the proof without really increasing heights

- for the quantifier cuts we eliminate one of those by at most doubling the height

- in the cut elimination we may copy parts of the proof and therefore may multiply the number of cuts

- we are therefore careful that we eliminate cuts in such a way that only smaller cuts are copied

- we can eliminate all cuts of highest rank by working from the top of the proof downwards — no new cuts of highest rank will be introduced in the process

- the estimate of height is given by a recursion over the height of the original proof — at each step we at most double the height of the subtree, and therefore get at most an exponential growth of the original height

- we decrease the cut rank, and get an exponential growth of the original height. By repeating this process and lowering the cut ranks to get rid of all cuts we get a super exponential growth of the original height

Note the following

- the cuts are eliminated in a specific order — starting with a topmost cut of maximal rank

- we need extra arguments to conclude that we could have eliminated cuts in a different order

1.4 ϵ-calculus

In the development of classical proof theory the ϵ-calculus of Hilbert played a special role. He introduced to every formula Ax a term $\epsilon x.Ax$ with the idea that it stood for a solution to

Ax if there was one solution. The syntax is straightforward — we start with literals and build up compound formulas with connectives. The ϵ-terms will then give new literals and from them new ϵ-terms and so on. We define quantifiers:

- $\exists x.Ax = A(\epsilon x.Ax)$

- $\forall x.Ax = A(\epsilon x.\neg Ax)$

Hilbert thought that ϵ-terms where ideal objects which could be eliminated — if there where a derivation $\vdash B$ of a formula B not containing any ϵ-terms, then we could also eliminate ϵ-terms from the derivation. This was proved for ordinary first order logic — and the hope was to do it also for stronger systems treating arithmetic. After Gentzens treatment of cut elimination in first order arithmetic Wilhelm Ackermann gave a proof of ϵ-elimination essentially involving arguments like Gentzens. We shall come back to this later.

1.5 Other systems

All the systems above are easily transferred to logics with $=$, to many sorted calculus and to infinitary calculus. The many sorted calculi is only a matter of more book keeping. We must keep track of the sorts. This is left to the reader. For our development the infinitary calculi is more interesting. The two most important are

Countable conjunctions and disjunctions: We then have
  as rules

$$\frac{\Gamma, F_k, \bigvee_i F_i}{\Gamma, \bigvee_i F_i} \; \bigvee$$

and

$$\frac{\cdots \;\; \Gamma, F_j \;\; \cdots}{\Gamma, \bigwedge_i F_i} \; \bigwedge$$

ω-**logic:**   The quantifiers are supposed to run over some countable data structure as for example natural numbers. We replace the quantifiers with the appropriate countable conjunctions and disjunctions.

The completeness of the cut-free calculus goes through as before and also the cut elimination argument — there is only a little extra work to make the processes fair.

We note that the connectives are supposed to be countable. The reason for this is that the (cut-free) calculus is simply not complete for uncountable connectives. Consider the valid formula

$$\bigwedge_{i \in \omega} \bigvee_{j \in 2} Aij \rightarrow \bigvee_{f \in 2^\omega} \bigwedge_{i \in \omega} Aifi$$

Assume that we have a cut-free derivation of it. This derivation is a wellfounded tree with countable branching. It only involves a countable number of instances of the rule $\bigvee$. That means that there is a countable subset F of 2^ω such that

$$\bigwedge_{i\in\omega}\bigvee_{j\in 2} Aij \rightarrow \bigvee_{f\in F}\bigwedge_{i\in\omega} Aifi$$

is derivable. But this formula is not valid as a simple diagonalization argument shows.

In our falsification procedure we get the term universe in a dynamic way. We get new eigen parameters as we go on in constructing the falsification tree. New eigen parameters are introduced in the analysis of $\forall$, and if we falsify an $\exists\forall$-combination we get a process where we construct an infinite number of eigen parameters. Of course we could have given the term universe in advance. This is — from a falsification point of view — what we do with Skolem functions. We leave to the reader to explore the connection.

Above we did not use use cut in our falsification procedure. We proved completeness for the cut free rules. But look a little closer at the proof. Our falsification is constructed from an open and fair branch in our falsification tree. The falsification comes from assigning false to all literals occurring in the branch. This is sufficient to get that all formulas in the branch are assigned false. But the falsification does not need to assign truth values to all atomic formulas. The falsification is usually partial.

On the other hand we could have used cuts in our falsification procedure. Let us use all possible cuts in a fair way — for each cut formula sooner or later it is used in every branch which does not stop. If we then have an open and fair branch, then the falsification is total. For every formula F : F is false in the falsification if and only if F is in the branch.

Given a theory T and a proof that it is consistent, then we can use the falsification procedure to get an open and fair branch in the falsification tree which gives a simple model M for T.

1.6   Infinitary proofs

So far the proofs are finite syntactic objects. They are used to describe provability. But as we have seen from Gödels incompleteness theorem there is a gap between provability and truth if the universe is one of the common data structures like pairs. By relaxing on the definition of proofs we are able to define truth in a "proof like" way. So assume we have a fixed universe $\mathcal{U}$. Then truth for sentences are defined by an AND-OR tree where at each node we have a sentence in negation normal form (negations innermost)

Conjunction: analyzed by a binary AND-branching

Disjunction: analyzed by a binary OR-branching

For all: analyzed by an AND-branching over each element in $\mathcal{U}$

Exists: analyzed by an OR-branching over each element in $\mathcal{U}$

This is just another way to write down the semantics of sentences — and gives exactly the same. Using sequents we can get rid of the OR-branchings provided

- The sequents are interpreted as finite disjunctions of sentences

- We analyze "exists" within a sequent using a fair procedure

The analysis of exists is done by:

$$\frac{\Gamma, \exists x. Fx, Fu}{\Gamma, \exists x. Fx}$$

The fairness of the procedure consists in that to every element $v \in \mathcal{U}$ sooner or later $\exists x. Fx$ must be analyzed as $\exists x. Fx, Fv$. This is always possible if the universe $\mathcal{U}$ is countable.

For countable universes we have sequential calculi with completeness and cut elimination. The argument for the finitary case is transferred in a direct way to the infinitary case.

Gentzen games

2.1 Gentzen trees

Our cut elimination works only from the top and downwards. We introduce the Gentzen trees as a way to see the combinatorics involved in the cut elimination and also at the same time prove that we get termination if we eliminate the cuts in any other order. The Gentzen trees are finite trees with unary and binary branching and natural numbers at the nodes. So an example could be

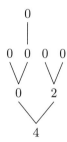

The tree structure corresponds to the proof structure, the numbers is the complexity of the cut and nodes with 0 on correspond to a rule different from a cut. So in the Gentzen trees we represent the height and the rank of a cut proof in a direct way.

2.2   Syntactic moves

The cut elimination is done by syntactic moves on proofs. Here
we do similar moves on the Gentzen trees. There are four types
of moves **A B C D**

Assumption: Reducing a cut number

Basic: Moving a cut upwards

Cut: Replacing a cut with simpler cuts

Deletion: Go to subtrees

To simplify the description we write down only the moves
on the left hand side, and also only the move involving the root.
We have also moves on the right hand side and moves on any
subtree.

A-move

At any node we can replace the number $n+1$ with n. Using the
A-move we can transform any Gentzen tree to a tree with only
0 at the nodes, but this is of course uninteresting.

B-move

Unary:

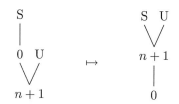

Binary:

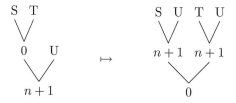

This is the move involved when we push a cut upwards in a proof. This can be done in many ways, especially when the cut formula is only a side formula in the rule above. Here is an example

$$\dfrac{\dfrac{A, F \qquad B, F}{A \land B, F} \qquad G, \neg F}{A \land B, G}$$

$$\mapsto$$

$$\frac{\dfrac{A,F \qquad G,\neg F}{A,G} \qquad \dfrac{B,F \qquad G,\neg F}{B,G}}{A \wedge B, G}$$

C-move

Now we get to the more interesting move — those changing the cuts in an essential way. The general rule is as follows

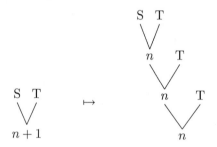

Here we have written the move with 3 copies of

In general we can repeat it an arbitrary number of times — from 0 and upwards. There are some limitations on the number of copies. This correspond to the Gentzen games for different logics

Propositional: A fixed number of copies. It is sufficient to
   have 2 copies.

Predicate: The number is bound by the height of S

Arithmetic: No bound. In Peano arithmetic you are only al-
   lowed to use this C-move at first on a node. Afterwards
   you must use the predicate version of the move on the
   node.

D-move

$$
\begin{array}{ccc}
\begin{array}{c} S \\ | \\ n \end{array} & \mapsto & S
\end{array}
$$

$$
\begin{array}{ccc}
\begin{array}{c} S \quad T \\ \bigvee \\ n \end{array} & \mapsto & S \text{ and } T
\end{array}
$$

After having introduced these moves the crucial questions
are after having started with a Gentzen tree

- Will any sequence of moves make it terminate?

- Is the partial ordering induced by the moves well founded?

Theorem 2.1 (Main theorem) *Any sequence of G-moves terminates.*

G-moves: Either A-, B-, C-, or D-move

G-ordering: Transitive closure of the moves

G-wellfounded: A Gentzen-tree where all runs terminate

Goal: To prove that all Gentzen-trees are G-wellfounded

Lemma 2.2 *If S and T are G-wellfounded, then so are*

$$
\begin{array}{ccc}
S & & S \quad T \\
\mid & and & \bigvee \\
n & & n
\end{array}
$$

Observe that the tree with only node m is wellfounded. So the lemma gives the main theorem. We prove the lemma by induction

Primary: The natural number n

Secondary: Either G-smaller S and same T or same S and G-smaller T

Induction: It is sufficient to prove that all results of one move on the Gentzen tree above is G-wellfounded

After one move we get one of

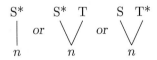

where S* is G-less than S and T* is G-less than T. In either case we get the trees G-wellfounded by secondary induction.

Consider typically the following C-move

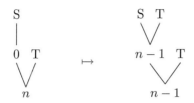

Secondary induction and then primary induction gives G-wellfounded

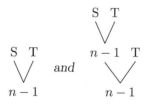

Propositional

Consider the transformations

- $\vdash \Gamma, F \wedge G \Rightarrow \vdash \Gamma, F$ and $\vdash \Gamma, G$

- $\vdash \Gamma, F \vee G \Rightarrow \vdash \Gamma, F, G$

They are proved by replacing $F \wedge G$ with F or with G, and $F \vee G$ with F, G within a thread in the derivation — starting at the conclusion and going upwards. This hardly changes the derivations — there may be two changes

- we may use a trivial step — conclusion and premiss is the same

- we may delete a branch

If we look at the corresponding Gentzen trees, they are connected by G-moves.

The typical NP-complete problem is of the form

- Given a problem $\mathcal{P}(n)$ with parameter n

- Construct (polynomially in n) a binary tree $\mathcal{T}(n)$ with height polynomial in n

- Is there a branch satisfying some simple property ?

Satisfiability in propositional logic is of this form. Validity is CO-NP.

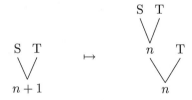

This move keeps us within trees with height polynomial. With height h and maximal cut degree n we get to a cut free proof of height less than

$$2^n \cdot h$$

and are therefore within trees of polynomial height for each fixed n in the cut eliminations using propositional C-moves.

Predicate

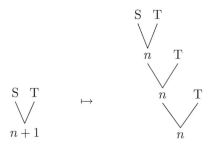

The difference between the various logics are the number of iterations of

In propositional logic we had a fixed number of iterations — the number can be taken to be 2. In predicate logic the

number of iterations is bound by the height of S. In arithmetic we only know that the number of iterations is finite. First order arithmetic is a mixture — in the first C-move on a node we can have any finite number of iterations, but from then on the bound of iterations for C-moves on that node is bound as in predicate logic.

Observe that we can perform the cut transformation in predicate logic using predicate C-moves to have enough subtrees to be substituted and then use B-moves to get the cuts in the appropriate places.

Arithmetic

In sequential calculus we use the induction rule

$$\frac{\Gamma, F0 \quad \Delta, \neg Fa, Fa'}{\Gamma, Ft, \Delta}$$

There are two ways the rule can be broken down

- We embed the derivations into ω-logic. Then we transform the finite trees into trees with infinite branching. The theory above go through with the appropriate changes.

- We only break down the induction rule for the case where the term t is a natural number. In general t may contain free variables. But for proving consistency of arithmetic it is sufficient to consider inductions where the induction term is a number.

In both cases the rule is transformed to a sequence of cuts and we can use the G-moves. Note that in both cases we use the induction C-move on a node only once and from then on we use the predicate C-move.

2.3 Strong termination

In the Gentzen games we have strong termination — any sequence of moves terminate. This transforms to sequential calculus — any sequence of cut-elimination moves terminate. In particular we may start with the moves from the bottom of the derivation and upwards. Note the following

- To every cut transformation in sequent calculus there correspond a sequemce of moves in the Gentzen game — but not conversely

- The formulas in the sequent calculus tell us which moves to take

3

Ordinals

3.1 Well Orderings

> It must be conceded that Cantor's set theory, and
> in particular his creation of ordinals, is a grandiose
> mathematical idea. *Thoralf Skolem*

An ordinal is the order type of a wellordered set. The simplest ordinals are the natural numbers

$$0, 1, 2, 3, 4, 5, \ldots$$

Beyond that we have ω which we can visualize as follows

The order type is the same if we put a big circle before

but not if we put it after

In the first case we have $1 + \omega = \omega$, while in the second case we have $\omega + 1 > \omega$

3.2   Arithmetical operations

We can obviously construct some ordinals. The ordinal ω is given by the natural numbers. Addition is performed by putting one ordering after the other:

$$A + B \quad : \quad \underline{}^{A} \ \underline{}^{B} \quad A \text{ then } B$$

Multiplication is done by using the lexicographical ordering of pairs:

$$A \times B \quad : \quad \underbrace{\overset{AAA}{|||} \cdots \overset{A}{|}}_{B} \quad A \text{ copied } B \text{ times}$$

Addition and multiplication is the same for cardinals and ordinals. Cardinal exponentiation is defined by using all functions, while ordinal exponentiation is defined by all functions with finite support. So to define ω^A we consider functions $f : A \to \omega$ with $fa = 0$ for all but a finite number of the a's. The graphs of such functions are ordered lexicographically — the values of the larger a's being more important.

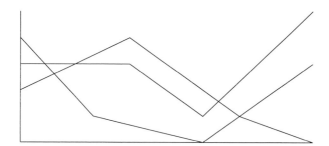

Note that we define the arithmetical operation without invoking that the orderings are well ordered. For the exponentiation we could have defined B^A as long as B has a least element.

With the arithmetical operations on ordinals we get up to the ordinal ε_0 which is defined by

$$
\begin{aligned}
\alpha_1 &= \omega + 1 \\
\alpha_{n+1} &= 2^{\alpha_n} \\
\varepsilon_0 &= \sup_n \alpha_n
\end{aligned}
$$

$\varepsilon_0 = 2^{2^{\cdot^{\cdot^{\omega+1}}}}$ can be seen as the order type of finitely many times iterated (inverse) lexicographical ordering. Tranfinite induction on it is an iteration of the ordinary induction over (inverse) lexicographical ordering.

3.3   Delayed decisions

Let us give one of the simplest examples where we use the ordinals. Consider the following one-person game. We have given

- some boxes — say five boxes

- the boxes are ordered from right to left

- in each box there is a finite number of balls

- a move in the game consists in taking away one ball from a box — and put a finite number of balls in some of the boxes to the right

- the game terminates if there are no balls left in any of the boxes

Obviously this game will always terminate. A way to prove this is to assign each configuration of boxes and balls an ordinal number less than ω^5 — if there are 3, 2, 0, 1, 8 balls in the 5 boxes we assign the ordinal

$$\omega^4 \cdot 3 + \omega^3 \cdot 2 + \omega \cdot 1 + 8$$

and each move will lower the assigned ordinal. The indeterminacy of the moves does not matter. This gives a way to treat delayed decisions.

Many of our proof theoretic analyses are like this box-and-ball game. In particular we note the treatment of delayed decisions. When we start we do not know all the moves. We have not decided how many balls to put in the boxes after having one ball removed. This is not something we can calculate — we simply do not know. In the ball-and-box game there is no way we can calculate the number of moves the game will take. In applications to computations we often distinguish between compile-time and run-time properties. Here the distinction is very clear.

We could analyze primitive recursive computations with a box-and-ball game with a finite number of boxes. Here we have a computation of for-loops nested within for-loops. The critical thing is that we first know when we enter a for-loop how many times we shall enter into it. We get a distinction between knowledge compile-time and knowledge run-time. The knowledge run-time is analyzed as if they were delayed decisions in a box-and-ball game.

Transfinite induction

4

4.1 Transfinite induction

We can obviously represent the ordinals — say below ε_0 — by some syntactical formulation. We suppose this is done in the language, and just write the ordinals instead of their representation. For our purposes in this chapter this is straightforward. We can then define transfinite induction for some formula F up to some ordinal α by

$$
\begin{aligned}
\mathbf{PROG}(F) &: \quad \forall\beta(\forall\gamma < \beta F(\gamma) \to F(\beta)) \\
\mathbf{TI}(\alpha, F) &: \quad \mathbf{PROG}(F) \to \forall\beta < \alpha F(\beta) \\
\mathbf{TI}(\alpha) &: \quad \mathbf{TI}(\alpha, F) \text{ for all } F
\end{aligned}
$$

The first property is called progressive. The property of being progressive subsumes the usual assumption in induction formulated as a course of values induction. $\mathbf{TI}(\omega, F)$ corresponds to induction over natural numbers and is provable in Peano arithmetic. We now want to prove that transfinite induction is closed under addition, multiplication and exponentiation. This is done by taking transfinite induction over some more complicated properties.

Simple properties:

- $\mathbf{TI}(\omega)$ — this is ordinary induction

- $\mathbf{TI}(\beta) \wedge \alpha < \beta \to \mathbf{TI}(\alpha)$ — we represent the ordinals in a primitive recursive way

Addition. $\mathbf{TI}(\alpha) \wedge \mathbf{TI}(\beta) \to \mathbf{TI}(\alpha + \beta)$. So assume we have

$$\mathbf{PROG}(F)$$

By $\mathbf{TI}(\alpha, F)$ we get

$$\forall x < \alpha . F(x)$$

But then $\mathbf{PROG}(\lambda x. F(\alpha + x))$.
By $\mathbf{TI}(\beta, \lambda x. F(\alpha + x))$ we get

$$\forall x < \beta . F(\alpha + x)$$

and hence

$$\forall x < \alpha + \beta . F(x)$$

We get $\mathbf{TI}(\alpha + \beta, F)$ from $\mathbf{TI}(\alpha, F)$ and $\mathbf{TI}(\beta, \lambda x. F(\alpha + x))$.

Multiplication. $\mathbf{TI}(\alpha) \wedge \mathbf{TI}(\beta) \to \mathbf{TI}(\alpha \times \beta)$.
So assume $\mathbf{PROG}(F)$, $\beta_0 < \beta$ and $\forall x < \alpha \times \beta_0 . F(x)$.
Using the assumption we get $\mathbf{PROG}(\lambda x. F(\alpha \times \beta_0 + x))$
and by $\mathbf{TI}(\alpha, \lambda x. F(\alpha \times \beta_0 + x))$ we get

$$\forall x < \alpha . F(\alpha \times \beta_0 + x)$$

This gives $\mathbf{PROG}(\lambda y. F(\alpha \times y))$ and using

$$\mathbf{TI}(\beta, \lambda y.F(\alpha \times y))$$

we get $\forall z < \alpha \times \beta.F(z)$.

We prove $\mathbf{TI}(\alpha \times \beta, F)$ using $\mathbf{TI}(\alpha, \lambda x.F(\alpha \times \beta_0 + x))$ and $\mathbf{TI}(\beta, \lambda y.F(\alpha \times y))$.

2-Exponentiation. We want to prove $\mathbf{TI}(\alpha) \to \mathbf{TI}(2^\alpha)$

For the proof we need the following easily proved fact about ordinals

$$\gamma + \beta < \gamma + 2^\alpha \Rightarrow \exists \alpha_0 < \alpha.\gamma + \beta < \gamma + 2^{\alpha_0} \times 3$$

Consider the more abstract property

$$F^*(x) : \forall y.(\forall z < y.F(z) \to \forall z < y + 2^x.F(z))$$

We first prove

$$\mathbf{PROG}(F) \to \mathbf{PROG}(F^*)$$

So let $\mathbf{PROG}(F)$, α and $\forall x < \alpha.F^*(x)$ be given.

We want to prove $F^*(\alpha)$.

Let β and $\forall z < \beta.F(z)$ be given.

We want to prove $\forall z < \beta + 2^\alpha.F(z)$.

Let $\gamma < \beta + 2^\alpha$ be given.

There is $\alpha_0 < \alpha$ with $\gamma < \beta + 2^{\alpha_0} \times 3$.

Using $F^*(\alpha_0)$ we get $\forall y.(\forall z < y.F(z) \to \forall z < y + 2^{\alpha_0}.F(z))$.

Applying it three times we get

$$\forall y.(\forall z < y.F(z) \to \forall z < y + 2^{\alpha_0} + 2^{\alpha_0} + 2^{\alpha_0} = y + 2^{\alpha_0} \times 3.F(z))$$

Therefore we have proved $F(\gamma)$, $\forall z < \beta + 2^{\alpha}.F(z)$, $F^*(\alpha)$ and $\mathbf{PROG}(F^*)$.

Now we prove

$$\mathbf{TI}(\alpha, F^*) \to \mathbf{TI}(2^{\alpha}, F)$$

So assume $\mathbf{TI}(\alpha, F^*)$ and $\mathbf{PROG}(F)$. Then $\mathbf{PROG}(F^*)$ and we get

$$\forall x < \alpha.F^*(x)$$

and $F^*(\alpha)$ which is

$$\forall y.(\forall z < y.F(z) \to \forall z < y + 2^{\alpha}, F(z))$$

Substituting $y = 0$ we get

$$\forall z < 2^{\alpha}.F(z)$$

and the proof is finished.

Note. Observe that the proofs reflect the geometric structure we used in defining the arithmetical operations. The proof of addition can be broken into two pieces — first we prove induction up to α, then the stretch from α to $\alpha + \beta$. In multiplication we have a nesting — an outer proof along α and then for each point inside a proof of β. Exponentiation must be explained by the more abstract property we also used in explaining what exponentiation of ordinals were.

Discussion. We have proved that transfinite induction over ordinals are closed under the usual arithmetical operations. This gets us up to every ordinal less than ε_0. For addition and multiplication we only need to have induction over some slightly more complicated predicates. The big step is with the exponentiation. Observe that we get transfinite induction over exponentiation by having extra quantifiers in the new predicates. Here there is a tradeoff between using larger ordinals and having more complicated induction formulas.

4.2 Ordinal bounds

We now want to do two different things

- in this section we show that the ordinal ϵ_0 occur as a bound for heights when we eliminate cuts in infinitary calculus

- in the next section we show that ϵ_0 is a bound for the transfinite induction we can prove in arithmetic

We try to make the argument robust — the details involved can be done in many ways. We have a sequential calculus with an ω-rule

$$\frac{\Gamma, F0 \quad \Gamma, F1 \quad \Gamma, F2 \quad \ldots}{\Gamma, \forall x.Fx}$$

As usual we have a cut rule which we try to eliminate in derivations

$$\frac{\Gamma, F \quad \Gamma, \neg F}{\Gamma}$$

This elimination increases the height of the derivation. In the elimination procedure we look at

- the height of the derivation

- the cut ranks — that is the nesting of quantifiers in the cut formulas

The procedure works in many passes. In each pass we start from the top of the derivation and works downwards. In the first pass we eliminate cuts with maximal rank, in the next pass cuts with second highest rank and so on. Now we have the following observations

- we can eliminate outermost conjunctions and disjunctions in a cutformula with just slightly increase of height

- we can eliminate outermost quantifier in a cutformula which is topmost and with maximal rank with at most a doubling of the height

- we can eliminate atomic cuts

The crucial elimination is the one for the quantifiers. Let us repeat how this is done. We start with a cut

$$\frac{\Gamma, \exists x.Fx \quad \Delta, \forall x.\neg Fx}{\Gamma, \Delta}$$

We first observe that we have the following transformation for universal quantifier

$$\vdash \Delta, \forall x.\neg Fx \Rightarrow\vdash \Delta, \neg Ft \text{ where } t \text{ is any term}$$

and that this transformation neither increase the height nor the cut rank of the derivation. This is simply proved by induction over the height. We now look at the existential quantifier. A typical derivation of $\Gamma, \exists x.Fx$ looks like

$$
\begin{array}{c}
\dfrac{\Gamma_1, Fs}{\Gamma_1, \exists x.Fx} \\
\vdots
\end{array}
\qquad
\begin{array}{c}
\dfrac{\Gamma_3, Fu}{\Gamma_3, \exists x.Fx} \\
\vdots \\
\dfrac{\Gamma_2, \exists x.Fx, Ft}{\Gamma_2, \exists x.Fx} \\
\vdots \\
\Gamma, \exists x.Fx
\end{array}
$$

We now replace the $\exists x.Fx$ with Δ and inferences of $\exists x.Fx$ with some cuts with cut rank the rank of Ft

$$\frac{\Gamma_3, Fu \quad \Delta, \neg Fu}{\Gamma_3, \Delta}$$

$$\frac{\Gamma_1, Fs \quad \Delta, \neg Fs}{\Gamma_1, \Delta} \qquad \vdots$$

$$\vdots \qquad \frac{\Gamma_2, \Delta, Ft \qquad \Delta, \neg Ft}{\Gamma_2, \Delta}$$

$$\vdots$$

$$\Gamma, \Delta$$

The cut rank is not increased, but as height we may get the sum of the two heights. It was necessary here to consider topmost cut of maximal rank. We put in many copies of the inferences involving $\Delta, \forall x.\neg Fx$ and we must be sure that they do not contain cutformulas of higher rank. Here we eliminate a topmost cut of maximal rank.

We eliminate all cuts of maximal rank by increasing the height exponentially $\alpha \mapsto 2^\alpha$. Then we have to make new passes for the second highest rank, the third highest rank and so on. For each pass we get an exponential jump in the height. If the original derivation was of infinite height but less than ε_0, then the cutfree derivation is of height $< \varepsilon_0$.

We now come to arithmetic. We use ω-logic to handle induction. Let us say we have an arithmetical system with induction

$$\frac{F0 \quad \forall y.(\neg Fy \vee Fsy)}{\forall x.Fx}$$

We can replace it with an instance of the ω-rule and many cuts

$$
\cfrac{F0 \quad \cfrac{\neg F0, F1 \quad \cfrac{\cfrac{F0 \quad \neg F0, F1}{F1} \quad \neg F1, F2}{F2}}{F1} \quad \cdots}{\forall x.Fx}
$$

This transforms a derivation in first order arithmetic of finite height and finite cut rank into a derivation of finite cut rank and height $< \omega^2$. After cutelimination we get a derivation of height $< \varepsilon_0$. We leave to the reader to get more exact estimates.

4.3   Bounds for provable transfinite induction

Transfinite induction is given by

$$
\mathbf{PROG}(F) : \forall x.(\forall y < x.Fy \rightarrow Fx)
$$

$$
\mathbf{TI}(\alpha, F) : \mathbf{PROG}(F) \rightarrow \forall x < \alpha.Fx
$$

Let us now assume that we have a system for first order arithmetic with ordinals and one special predicate letter F. We have shown that we are able to prove

$$
\mathbf{TI}(\alpha, F) \text{ where } \alpha < \varepsilon_0
$$

In this section we shall prove that we cannot do better. To do this we introduce a new system with the following infinitary rule, called progressionrule, for each ordinal α

$$\frac{F0 \quad F1 \quad \ldots \quad F\beta \quad \ldots}{F\alpha} \qquad \text{where } \beta < \alpha$$

In this system **PROG**(F) is derivable. Furthermore the system with ω-rule and progressionrule admits cut elimination and the estimates of height are the same. The only place where the new rule can be involved in cuts are with atomic cuts and cutformula F.

Assume now that we have proved in the ordinary first order theory

$$\textbf{TI}(\alpha, F)$$

Then we can imbed this derivation into the system with ω-rule and progressionrules. There we can derive

$$F\alpha$$

This derivation is of height $< \omega^2$ and of finite cut rank. The cut elimination gives a cutfree derivation of height $< \varepsilon_0$. Now look at such a cut free derivation of $F\alpha$. This derivation can only contain progressionrules and we see that α must be less or equal to its height. Therefore

$$\alpha < \varepsilon_0$$

This is interesting. It gives us a concrete Gödel sentence. The sentence **TI**(ε_0, F) is not provable in first order arithmetic — and we can state Gentzens result.

Theorem 4.1 (Gentzen) $\vdash_{PA} TI(\alpha) \Leftrightarrow \alpha < \epsilon_0$

The two sides combine different worlds

Left: Provability in first order arithmetic

Right: Ordertype of α is less than iterated lexicographical ordering

And the proof involves

$\Rightarrow$: The complexity of a direct proof of $TI(\alpha)$

$\Leftarrow$: Provability of transfinite induction is closed under exponentiation

Gentzens result is an improvement over Gödels incompleteness. It analyzes provability in a system using the mathematical statement $\alpha < \epsilon_0$.

4.4 Arithmetical systems

These are logical systems over the data structure unary numbers $\mathcal{N}$. We have start $0 : \mathcal{N}$ and successor $' : \mathcal{N} \to \mathcal{N}$ and less than $< : \mathcal{N} \times \mathcal{N} \to \textbf{BOOL}$. On the top of that there may be defined some other operations. For the coding in Gödels incompleteness theorem we need at least addition and multiplication. For other data structures we need less. On the top of that we have some levels of systems. The most important is.

Basic arithmetic: As axioms we have all true Δ_0 sentences. The truth values of these can be decided in PSPACE.

Robinson arithmetic: A slight strengthening of basic arithmetic with a finite set of axioms.

Skolem arithmetic: We include induction over quantifier free formulas.

Peano arithmetic: We have induction over arbitrary formulas.

We have similar levels for formal systems over any data structure. Beyond these levels we have levels where we define new relations using inductive definitions. More about this later.

5

Quantifiers

5.1 Skolem and quantifiers

With quantifiers we can express complicated properties with almost no effort. This is of course both good and bad news. The good news is that the language is very expressive. The bad news is that there are almost no new information involved.

Thoralf Skolem was especially concerned with the role of the quantifiers. He introduced (his variant of) the analyzing tree with new names introduced for the $\forall$-quantifiers and the $\exists$-quantifiers as source for terms. In this way he proved the mathematical core of the completeness theorem in 1922. He was also the first to prove that in some cases quantifiers could be eliminated. In 1919 he read Russell & Whiteheads "Principia Mathematica". He disagreed with the claims there for having made a foundation for mathematics. Instead he sketched in 1923 an alternative foundation. He introduced

- a rich system of terms — the primitive recursive functions

- a logic for proving properties of such terms — quantifier-free arithmetic

This was used to give a development of arithmetic. In more modern terms we could say that he introduced simultaneously a programming language and a programming logic. Both for the first time. The programming language was the language of primitive recursive functions. The logic is interesting here. He had free variable statements like we are used to in mathematics

$$a + b \;=\; b + a$$

and for the proofs he used the induction rule

$$\vdash F0 \,,\, \vdash Fa \to Fa' \Rightarrow \vdash Ft$$

with the predicate Fa quantifierfree but could contain other free variables. This way of thinking is of course quite close to mathematical practice — and in my opinion Skolem made a very good point against Russell & Whitehead.

In a free variable theory we can interpret some quantifier combinations. The statement

$$\forall x.Fx$$

corresponds to

$$Fa$$

with a a free variable. And

$$\forall x.\exists y.Gxy$$

corresponds to

$$Ga\phi a$$

for some free variable a and some term ϕa .

Skolem worked both in number theory and logic. One of his first insights in logic comes from number theory. In Diophantine equations we can reduce the degree to 2 by adding new variables and equations. Say we have the equation

$$y = x^5$$

Then we can introduce new variables u, v and equations

$$u = x^2$$
$$v = u^2$$
$$y = vx$$

And we can get down to a single equation in degree 4 by introducing the sum of squares

$$(u - x^2)^2 + (v - u^2)^2 + (y - vx)^2 = 0$$

Skolem used a similar trick to reduce the quantifier complexity by introducing new relation symbols. Say we have a sentence

$$\forall x.\exists y.\forall u.\exists v.Rxyuv$$

We can replace it by the conjunctions of universal quantifications using new relation symbols S, T, U

$$(Sxyu \leftrightarrow \exists v.Rxyuv) \wedge (Txy \leftrightarrow \forall u.Sxyu) \wedge (Ux \leftrightarrow \exists y.Txy) \wedge \forall x.Ux$$

In this way we can reduce sentences to $\forall\exists$-form. This simplified form was used by Skolem in giving procedures for falsifying sentences and getting the mathematical core of the completeness theorem for predicate calculus.

5.2   Gödels interpretation

In 1942 Kurt Gödel introduced an interesting way of interpreting theories of arithmetic into quantifier free theories. Gödel lectured about the results, but is was forgotten and revived with a publication in 1958 in the journal Dialectica.

We go through Joseph Shoenfields variant of Gödels Dialectica interpretation. Then we'll go through some possible rules in arithmetic and see what kind of terms are needed for the corresponding quantifier free theory T. The terms in T are functionals of finite type over the type of natural numbers $\mathcal{N}$ — using primitive recursion also for higher order functionals. The theory T will be a free variable theory built on

- classical propositional calculus

- cutrule

- quantifier free induction

- equality in the ground type

- recursion equations for the terms introduced

Gödel used intuitionistic logic, but his interpretation works equally well in classical logic as Shoenfield showed. It becomes particularly simple if we restrict the logical language to the symbols $\neg$, $\wedge$, $\vee$ and $\forall$. In the development below we will go through the rules of arithmetic and show how the interpretation into $\mathcal{T}$ propagates starting from interpretation of axioms and the go from interpretation of premisses of rules to interpretation of their conclusion. As a result we get an interpretation for each sequent derivable in arithmetic.

First we must tell what an interpretation of a sequent in arithmetic is. To each formula F we assign a formula $F^{\#}$ of form

$$\forall a.\exists b.Rab$$

where Rab is a formula of $\mathcal{T}$ and a and b are functionals of higher type.

For atomic F

$$F^{\#} = F$$

Assume

$$F^{\#} = \forall a.\exists b.Rab$$
$$G^{\#} = \forall c.\exists d.Scd$$
$$Hx^{\#} = \forall e.\exists f.Tefx$$

Then

$$
\begin{aligned}
(\neg F)^{\#} &= \forall B.\exists a.\neg RaBa \\
(F \wedge G)^{\#} &= \forall ac.\exists bd.(Rab \wedge Scd) \\
(F \vee G)^{\#} &= \forall ac.\exists bd.(Rab \vee Scd) \\
(\forall x.Hx)^{\#} &= \forall ex.\exists f.Tefx
\end{aligned}
$$

Observe the way negation is treated. Here we go up in the type hierarchy. This has of course consequences for the treatment of existential quantifiers. Using the above we translate

$$
\begin{aligned}
&\exists a.\forall b.\exists c.R\; a\; b\; c \\
&\neg\forall a.\neg\forall b.\exists c.R\; a\; b\; c \\
&\neg\forall a.\forall C.\exists b.\neg R\; a\; b\; Cb \\
&\forall B.\exists a.\exists C.R\; a\; BaC\; C(BaC)
\end{aligned}
$$

In the above translation we delete all quantifiers which are not referred to. Using this we get that any formula of form $\forall\exists$ is translated as itself. Only with quantifier combination $\exists\forall$ do we get something new.

Now we show how to treat sequents. Consider — to simplify our explanation — the sequent $\Gamma = F, G$ with $F^{\#}$ and $G^{\#}$ as above. We say that Γ *can be interpreted in* $\mathcal{T}$ if there are terms ϕ and ψ such that

$$
\vdash_{\mathcal{T}} Ra\phi ac\,,\; Sc\psi ac
$$

Note that as arguments in both ϕ and ψ we may have all free variables in the sequent. We will also use the more compact notation

$$\vdash_{\mathcal{T}} Rab^\star \,,\, Scd^\star$$

where the $\star$ indicates that we have terms with variables from the free variables in the sequent. For sequents with more formulas we do the same as above.

5.3 The proof

Definition 5.1 *A rule is interpretable if from an interpretation of the premisses we get an interpretation of the conclusion. An axiom is interpretable if it can be interpreted.*

Theorem 5.2 *Axioms in arithmetic are interpretable.*

All literals — in fact all quantifierfree formulas — are interpreted by themselves. Axioms in arithmetic are transferred to axioms in $\mathcal{T}$. Now to the rules

Theorem 5.3 (Contraction) $\vdash_{\mathcal{T}} \Gamma, F, F \Rightarrow \vdash_{\mathcal{T}} \Gamma, F$ *is interpretable.*

Let $F^\# = \forall a.\exists b.Rab$. By assumption we have in $\mathcal{T}$

$$\vdash_{\mathcal{T}} \Pi, Rab^\star, Rcd^\star$$

where $b^\star = \phi ac$ and $d^\star = \psi ac$. Substitute c for a and define by cases

$$\xi a = \left\{ \begin{array}{ll} \phi aa & \text{if } Ra\phi aa \\ \psi aa & \text{if } \neg Ra\phi aa \end{array} \right.$$

Then

$$\vdash_T \Pi, Ra\xi a$$

Theorem 5.4 (Conjunction) $\vdash \Gamma, F \& \vdash \Gamma, G \Rightarrow \vdash \Gamma, F \wedge G$ *is interpretable.*

Assume that in T we have $\vdash_T \Pi, Rab^\star$ and $\vdash_T \Pi, Scd^\star$. Then

$$\vdash_T \Pi, Rab^\star \wedge Scd^\star$$

Theorem 5.5 (Negation-Conjunction) $\vdash \Gamma, \neg F \Rightarrow \vdash \Gamma, \neg(F \wedge G)$ *is interpretable.*

$$
\begin{aligned}
(\neg F)^\star &= \forall B.\exists a.\neg RaBa \\
(\neg(F \wedge G))^\star &= \forall B\, D.\exists ac.\neg(RaBac \wedge ScDac)
\end{aligned}
$$

We assume in T $\vdash_T \Pi, \neg Ra^\star Ba^\star$. But then for a freely chosen term $c^\star \vdash_T \Pi, \neg(Ra^\star Ba^\star \wedge Sc^\star Dc^\star)$. A similar argument for the case where we permute F and G.

Theorem 5.6 (Disjunction) $\vdash \Gamma, F \Rightarrow \vdash \Gamma, F \vee G$ *is interpretable.*

Similar to negation-conjunction.

Theorem 5.7 (Negation-disjunction) $\vdash \Gamma, \neg F \& \vdash \Gamma, \neg G \Rightarrow \vdash \Gamma, \neg(F \vee G)$ *is interpretable.*

Similar to conjunction.

Theorem 5.8 (Double negation) $\vdash \Gamma, F \Rightarrow \vdash \Gamma, \neg\neg F$ *is interpretable.*

$$
\begin{aligned}
F^\# &= \forall a.\exists b.R\,a\,b \\
(\neg F)^\# &= \forall B.\exists a.\neg R\,a\,Ba \\
(\neg\neg F)^\# &= \forall A.\exists B.\neg\neg R\,AB\,B(AB)
\end{aligned}
$$

Assume $\vdash_T \Pi, R\,a\,b^\star$ where $b^\star = \phi a$. Define $B^\star = \phi$ and substitute $A\phi$ for a. Then

$$
\begin{aligned}
&\vdash_T \Pi, R\,A\phi\,\phi(A\phi) \\
&\vdash_T \Pi, R\,AB^\star\,B^\star(AB^\star) \\
&\vdash_T \Pi, \neg\neg R\,AB^\star\,B^\star(AB^\star)
\end{aligned}
$$

Theorem 5.9 ($\forall$-quantifier) $\vdash \Gamma, Fa \Rightarrow \vdash \Gamma, \forall x.Fx$ *is interpretable.*

$$
\begin{aligned}
(Fa)^\# &= \forall b.\exists c.Rabc \\
(\forall x.Fx)^\# &= \forall a\,b.\exists c.Rabc
\end{aligned}
$$

Both are interpreted in the same way.

Theorem 5.10 (Negation-$\forall$) $\vdash \Gamma, \neg F\phi \Rightarrow \vdash \Gamma, \neg\forall x.Fx$ *is interpretable.*

$$
\begin{aligned}
(Fa)^{\#} &= \forall b_0.\exists c.R\,a\,b_0\,c \\
(\neg Fa)^{\#} &= \forall C.\exists b_0.\neg R\,a\,b_0\,Cb_0 \\
(\forall x.Fx)^{\#} &= \forall ab_1.\exists c.R\,a\,b_1\,c \\
(\neg \forall x.Fx)^{\#} &= \forall D.\exists ab_1.\neg R\,a\,b_1\,Dab_1
\end{aligned}
$$

We assume $\vdash_{\mathcal{T}} \Pi, \neg R\,\phi\,b_0^{\star}\,Cb_0^{\star}$. Then define $a^{\star} = \phi$ and $b_1^{\star} = b_0^{\star}$. Then substitute $\lambda b.Da^{\star}b$ for C to get $\vdash_{\mathcal{T}} \Pi, \neg R\,a^{\star}\,b_1^{\star}\,Da^{\star}b_1^{\star}$.

Theorem 5.11 (Cut) $\vdash \Gamma, F$ & $\vdash \Gamma, \neg F \Rightarrow \Gamma$ *is interpretable.*

$$
\begin{aligned}
F^{\#} &= \forall a \cdot \exists b \cdot R\,a\,b \\
(\neg F)^{\#} &= \forall B \cdot \exists a \cdot \neg R\,a\,Ba
\end{aligned}
$$

Assume $\vdash_{\mathcal{T}} \Pi, R\,a\,b^{\star}$ and $\vdash_{\mathcal{T}} \Pi, \neg R\,a^{\star}\,Ba^{\star}$ where $b^{\star}$ may contain a and the free variables of Π and $a^{\star}$ may contain B and the free variables of Π. We define $\phi = \lambda a.b^{\star}$ and $\psi = \lambda B.a^{\star}$. Both contain only free variables from Π. Substitute ϕ for B and $\psi\phi$ for a. Then

$$
\begin{aligned}
&\vdash_{\mathcal{T}} \Pi, R\,\psi\phi\,\phi(\psi\phi) \\
&\vdash_{\mathcal{T}} \Pi, \neg R\,\psi\phi\,\phi(\psi\phi) \\
&\vdash_{\mathcal{T}} \Pi
\end{aligned}
$$

Theorem 5.12 (Induction) $\vdash \Gamma, F0$ & $\vdash \Gamma, \neg Fa, Fsa \Rightarrow \vdash \Gamma, F\phi$ *is interpretable.*

$$(Fa)^{\#} \quad = \quad \forall b. \exists c. R\,a\,b\,c$$
$$\neg Fa)^{\#} \quad = \quad \forall C. \exists c. \neg R\,a\,b\,Cb$$

Assume $\vdash_{\mathcal{T}} \Pi, R\,0\,b_0\,c_0^{\star}$ and $\vdash_{\mathcal{T}} \Pi, \neg R\,a\,b^{\star}\,Cb^{\star}, R\,sa\,b_1\,c_1^{\star}$. Define $\phi = \lambda b_0.c_0^{\star}$, $\psi = \lambda aCb_1.b^{\star}$ and $\xi = \lambda aCb_1.c_1^{\star}$. Note that a is of type natural numbers.

We use it as recursion variable in defining ζ by primitive recursion

$$\zeta 0 \quad = \quad \phi$$
$$\zeta sa \quad = \quad \xi a s a$$

Note that the typing is correct. Substitute ζa for c and define $b^{\star\star} = \psi a(\zeta a)b_1$. Then

$$\vdash_{\mathcal{T}} \Pi, R\,0\,b\,\zeta 0 b$$
$$\vdash_{\mathcal{T}} \Pi, \neg R\,a\,b^{\star\star}\,\zeta ab^{\star\star}, R\,sa\,b\,\xi(\zeta a)b$$
$$\vdash_{\mathcal{T}} \Pi, \neg R\,a\,b^{\star\star}\,\zeta ab^{\star\star}, R\,sa\,b\,\zeta sab$$
$$\vdash_{\mathcal{T}} \Pi, R\,\phi\,b\,\zeta\phi b$$

This concludes the proof of

Theorem 5.13 (Dialectica interpretation) *Every sequent derivable in Peano arithmetic can be interpreted in Gödels $\mathcal{T}$.*

5.4 Discussion

There are three ingredients in Gödels interpretation

- the elementary arithmetical system $\mathcal{P}$

- the free variable system $\mathcal{T}$

- the primitive recursive terms of finite type

The system $\mathcal{P}$ is ordinary Peano arithmetic. Complicated quantifier combinations in $\mathcal{P}$ are traded off for complicated terms. Note that quantifier free formulas in $\mathcal{P}$ are interpreted by themselves and we do not need any new terms. This gives

Theorem 5.14 *Consistency of $\mathcal{T}$ implies consistency of $\mathcal{P}$.*

Gödel called his 1958 paper "Über eine bisher noch nicht benutzte Erweiterung des finiten Standpunktes." He thought — and many constructivists agreed — that the consistency of $\mathcal{T}$ is evident from a finite point of view.

Now look at $\mathcal{T}$ together with the term system. To interpret the rules of $\mathcal{P}$ we need some properties of $\mathcal{T}$. First of all we needed the properties of typed λ-calculus

- explicit definition

- definition by cases

- λ-abstraction

- composition

Then to the induction rule $\vdash_\mathcal{T} \Gamma, F0$ & $\vdash_\mathcal{T} \Gamma, \neg Fa, Fsa \Rightarrow$ $\vdash_\mathcal{T} \Gamma, F\phi$. The treatment of this depends on the quantifiers in Fa. There are three special cases

Quantifier free We do not need any special terms to interpret the rule.

Universal We do not need any special terms to interpret the rule.

Existential We need ordinary primitive recursive functions.

For the general case we need primitive recursive functionals of finite type.

Why use Gödels complicated interpretation of the quantifiers? One could have tried to interpret $\forall a.\exists b.F\,a\,b$ by a term B and $\forall a.F\,a\,Ba$ for all formulas F — and not only quantifier free formulas. From recursion theory we know that for quantifier free F we can assume that B is computable. But this is not longer true if F contains quantifiers.

Let Rab be quantifier free. Then

$$\vdash \forall a.\exists c.(\exists b\, Rab \to Rac)$$

Assume now that there is a term ϕ interpreting c. So

$$\vdash \forall a.(\exists b\, Rab \to Ra\,\phi a)$$

But obviously

$$\vdash \forall a.(\exists b\, Rab \leftarrow Ra\,\phi a)$$

and

$$\vdash \forall a.(\exists b \; Rab \leftrightarrow Ra \, \phi a)$$

But then ϕ cannot in general be computable — we do not have a computable way to decide whether $\exists b \; Rab$.

On the other hand there is a conceptually simpler interpretation than the one that Gödel gave. Georg Kreisel introduced the no counter example interpretation. Let F be an arithmetical formula in prenex form. In ordinary predicate logic we have $\vdash F \rightarrow F$. But then we can trade the $\forall$-quantifiers in the last F with function symbols $f_1, \ldots, f_m$ to get in predicate logic

$$\vdash F \rightarrow \exists y_1 \ldots y_n \cdot R f_1 \ldots f_m y_1 \ldots y_n$$

where R is quantifier free. Now assume in elementary arithmetic $\vdash_{\mathcal{A}} F$. Then

$$\vdash_{\mathcal{A}} \exists y_1 \ldots y_n \cdot R f_1 \ldots f_m y_1 \ldots y_n$$

The Gödel interpretation works equally well with the new function symbols. So there are terms $c_1^\star, \ldots, c_n^\star$ with

$$\vdash_{\mathcal{T}} R f_1 \ldots f_m c_1^\star \ldots c_n^\star$$

This is the no counter example interpretation. The new function symbols works as giving possible counterexamples as we noted in the previous chapter. Let us give two examples

$$
\begin{aligned}
F &= \exists x \forall y \exists z \cdot Rxyz \\
G &= \forall x \exists y \forall z \cdot Sxyz
\end{aligned}
$$

with R and S quantifier free. They are then interpreted as

$$\exists xz \cdot R\,x\,f\!x\,z$$
$$\exists y \cdot S\,g\,y\,hy$$

And if $\vdash_{\mathcal{A}} F$ and $\vdash_{\mathcal{A}} G$, then

$$\vdash_T R\,a^\star\,f\!a^\star\,c^\star$$
$$\vdash_T R\,g\,b^\star\,hb^\star$$

The interpreting terms $a^\star$ and $c^\star$ depend on the free variable f, and the interpreting term $b^\star$ depends on the free variables g and h.

5.5   Spectors interpretation

In 1960 Clifford Spector generalized Gödels interpretation to full second order arithmetic. Per Martin-Löf has given the following version.

Theorem 5.15 (Spector) $\vdash \Gamma, \forall a.\exists b.R\,a\,b \Rightarrow \vdash \Gamma, \exists f.\forall a.R\,a\,f\!a$ *where a is of type natural number is interpretable.*

$$
\begin{aligned}
(Rab)^{\#} &= \forall c.\exists d.S\,a\,b\,c\,d \\
(\forall a.\exists b.Rab)^{\#} &= \forall a\,C_0.\exists b\,D_0.S\,a\,b\,C_0 bD_0\,D_0(C_0 bD_0) \\
(\exists f.\forall a.Rab)^{\#} &= \forall A\,C_1.\exists f\,D_1.S\,A\!f D_1\,f(A\!f D_1)\,C_1 f D_1\,D_1(A\!f D_1)(C_1 f D_1)
\end{aligned}
$$

There are terms $b^\star$ and $D_0^\star$ such that

$$\vdash_T S \ a \ b^\star \ C_0 b^\star D_0^\star \ D_0^\star (C_0 b^\star D_0^\star)$$

Must find terms $f^\star$ and $D_1^\star$ such that

$$\vdash_T S \ Af^\star D_1^\star \ f^\star (Af^\star D_1^\star) \ C_1 f^\star D_1^\star \ D_1^\star (Af^\star D_1^\star)(C_1 f^\star D_1^\star)$$

using $b^\star$, $D_0^\star$ and appropriate substitutions of the free variables a and C_0. We must solve the equations

$$
\begin{aligned}
a &= Af^\star D_1^\star \\
b^\star &= f^\star (Af^\star D_1^\star) \\
C_0 b^\star D_0^\star &= C_1 f^\star D_1^\star \\
D_0^\star (C_0 b^\star D_0^\star) &= D_1^\star (Af^\star D_1^\star)(C_1 f^\star D_1^\star)
\end{aligned}
$$

It is sufficient to solve

$$
\begin{aligned}
a &= Af^\star D_1^\star \\
b^\star &= f^\star (Af^\star D_1^\star) \\
C_0 b^\star D_0^\star &= C_1 f^\star D_1^\star \\
D_0^\star &= D_1^\star (Af^\star D_1^\star)
\end{aligned}
$$

Introduce the pairs $e^\star = (b^\star, D_0^\star)$ and $g^\star = (f^\star, D_1^\star)$. Must solve

$$a = Ag^\star$$
$$e^\star = g^\star(Ag^\star)$$
$$C_0 e^\star = C_1 g^\star$$

Here a is of type natural number. We have given the term $e^\star$ with free variables a and C_0. Must find term $g^\star$ depending on A and C_1 and appropriate substitutions for a and C_0 such that the equations hold. We define $\epsilon = \lambda a C_0 \cdot e^\star$ and get

$$a = Ag^\star$$
$$\epsilon a C_0 = g^\star(Ag^\star)$$
$$C_0 e^\star = C_1 g^\star$$

The first equation have type $\mathcal{T}$. Say that the second have type π and the third have type σ. We then have the following types for the individual terms in the equations

$$a \;:\; \mathcal{N}$$
$$C_0 \;:\; \pi \to \sigma$$
$$\epsilon \;:\; \mathcal{N} \to ((\pi \to \sigma) \to \pi)$$
$$g^\star \;:\; \mathcal{N} \to \pi$$
$$A \;:\; (\mathcal{N} \to \pi) \to \mathcal{N}$$
$$C_1 \;:\; (\mathcal{N} \to \pi) \to \sigma$$

The $g^\star$ we want to find can then be seen as an infinite sequence of elements of type π. Let o be a constant of type π. We represent a finite sequence $(g_0, \ldots, g_{k-1})$ as the infinite sequence $(g_0, \ldots, g_{k-1}, o, o, o, \ldots)$. To solve the equations Spector defined the following auxiliary functional by bar recursion — abbreviating $g_0, \ldots, g_{a-1}$ by $\overline{g}$

$$\theta(\overline{g}) = \begin{cases} (\overline{g}) \text{ if } A(\overline{g}) < a \\ \theta(\overline{g}, \epsilon a(\lambda x \cdot C_1 \theta(\overline{g}, x))) \text{ otherwise} \end{cases}$$

Here θ is defined by the free variables A and C_1. These free variables are supposed to run over computable functionals. So sooner or later — by continuity of the computable functionals — the definition must terminate.

We then define

$$\begin{aligned} g^\star &= \theta() \\ a &= Ag^\star \\ C_0 &= \lambda x \cdot C_1 \theta(g_0, \ldots, g_{a-1}, x) \end{aligned}$$

and get a to be the number where the recursive definition of θ switches cases. We can now check that we have solutions of the equations

$$g^\star = \theta() = \theta(g_0) = \cdots = \theta(g_0, \ldots, g_a) = (g_0, \ldots, g_a)$$
$$g^\star(Ag^\star) = g^\star a = g_a = \epsilon a(\lambda x \cdot C_1 \theta(e_0, \ldots, e_{a-1}, x)) = \epsilon a C_0$$
$$C_0(\epsilon a C_0) = C_0 g_a = C_1 \theta(g_0, \ldots, g_{a-1}) = C_1 g^\star$$

5.6   ε-calculus

Another way to eliminate quantifiers in arithmetic is to use ε-calculus. We have a language of arithmetic (which includes 0 and $<$) extended with ε-terms. As new ε-axioms we have

$$Ar \rightarrow A\epsilon x.A \wedge \epsilon x.A \leq r$$

for any formula A. The quantifier free axioms are such that any closed ε-free term is equal to a numeral. As in predicate logic we have the ε-theorems.

Theorem 5.16 (First ε-theorem for arithmetic) *Any formula A in arithmetic is equivalent to a formula A^ϵ with no quantifiers and using ε-terms. A is provable in Peano-arithmetic if and only if A^ϵ is provable in ε-arithmetic.*

The only new thing is to prove that the induction rule is derivable from the ε-axioms. So assume that we have proved

$$\vdash F0 \wedge \forall x.(Fx \rightarrow Fsx)$$

Consider the term $t = \epsilon x.\neg Fx$. Then by the elementary axioms

$$\vdash t = 0 \vee \exists y.t = sy$$

We have

$$\vdash \epsilon x.\neg Fx = 0 \rightarrow F\epsilon x.\neg Fx$$

$$\vdash \epsilon x.\neg Fx = sy \land \neg Fy \rightarrow \epsilon x.\neg Fx \leq sy$$

$$\vdash \epsilon x.\neg Fx = sy \rightarrow Fy$$

$$\vdash \epsilon x.\neg Fx = sy \rightarrow F\epsilon x.\neg Fx$$

And then $\vdash F\epsilon x.\neg Fx$ — which corresponds to $\vdash \forall x.Fx$.

Theorem 5.17 (Second ϵ-theorem in arithmetic) *Let F be a formula without quantifiers, free variables or ϵ-terms. If F is provable with the ϵ-axioms, then it is provable without them.*

So assume we have a derivation of F not involving induction, but possibly involving ϵ-axioms. Let us list the ϵ-axioms involved

$$Ar_1\bar{y} \quad \rightarrow \quad A(\epsilon x.A)(\bar{y})\bar{y} \land (\epsilon x.A)(\bar{y}) \leq r_1$$
$$\ldots$$
$$Ar_m\bar{y} \quad \rightarrow \quad A(\epsilon x.A)(\bar{y})\bar{y} \land (\epsilon x.A)(\bar{y}) \leq r_m$$
$$Bs_1\bar{y} \quad \rightarrow \quad B(\epsilon x.B)(\bar{y})\bar{y} \land (\epsilon x.B)(\bar{y}) \leq s_1$$
$$\ldots$$
$$Bs_n\bar{y} \quad \rightarrow \quad B(\epsilon x.B)(\bar{y})\bar{y} \land (\epsilon x.B)(\bar{y}) \leq s_n$$
$$\ldots$$

In the derivation we get rid of all non-critical ϵ-terms (i e those not introduced by ϵ-axioms) and all free variables by substituting the constant 0 for them.

We assume that the ϵ-axioms are listed such that $\epsilon x.A$ is of highest rank, and then $\epsilon x.B$ etc. We observe then that in formula Ax there only occurs ϵ-terms introduced further down in the list. The same with Bx etc. There are of course no restriction on the ϵ-terms occuring in the terms $r_1, \ldots, r_m, s_1, \ldots, s_n, \ldots$

We now want to find substitutions of numerals for the ϵ-terms, $(\epsilon x.A)(\bar{y}) \mapsto \alpha(\bar{y})$, $(\epsilon x.B)(\bar{y}) \mapsto \beta(\bar{y})$, ... making all ϵ-axioms derivable. The substitution α can be regarded as a functional of the substitutions further down on the list. We put $\alpha(\bar{y}) = \alpha(\beta, \gamma, \ldots)(\bar{y})$ and $\beta(\bar{y}) = \beta(\gamma, \ldots)(\bar{y})$ etc.

Each $\alpha(\beta, \gamma, \ldots)(\bar{y})$ has two possible values — either 0 or the least x such that $Ax\bar{y}$. The one that is chosen depends on $Ax\bar{y}$ and on the finite list of ϵ-axioms used.

We first solve $\alpha(\beta, \gamma, \ldots)$ by successive approximations. To be pedantic we write $r\bar{y}\alpha\beta\gamma$ and $Ax\bar{y}\beta\gamma$ to indicate variables in the term r and the formula A. We then define

$$\alpha^0(\beta, \gamma)(\bar{y}) = 0$$

$$\alpha^{i+1}(\beta, \gamma)(\bar{y}) = \max(\alpha^i(\beta, \gamma)(\bar{y}), \mu x \leq \{r_1\bar{y}\alpha^i\beta\gamma, \ldots, r_m\bar{y}\alpha^i\beta\gamma\}Ax\bar{y}\beta\gamma)$$

$$\alpha^\infty = \lim \alpha^i$$

After having solved α, we then solve β by

$$\beta^0(\gamma)(\bar{y}) = 0$$

$$\beta^{i+1}(\gamma)(\bar{y}) = \max(\beta^i(\gamma)(\bar{y}), \mu x \leq \{r_1\bar{y}\alpha^\infty\beta^i\gamma, \ldots, r_m\bar{y}\alpha^\infty\beta^i\gamma\}Bx\bar{y}\gamma)$$

$$\beta^\infty = \lim \beta^i$$

and γ etc until we have given substitutions making all the ϵ-axioms derivable. We observe that $\alpha^\infty(\beta, \gamma)$ is continuous in β and γ and that $\beta^\infty(\gamma)$ is continuous in γ. This means that we can have the above as a simultaneous recursion of all the substitutions of the ϵ-terms.

Finite trees

6.1 Ordering trees

For the analysis of Gentzen we need to have a theory of ordinals with the ordinals less than ε_0 as a natural part. We do this here with finite trees. The trees are finite with finite branchings. The ordinals less than ε_0 turn out to be the trees with binary and unary branchings.

Instead of working with ordinals as something given and having names for some of them, we work directly with finite trees and give them an ordering which we show in a constructive way to be a well ordering.

The smallest tree is the one with just a root

$$\cdot \; = 0$$

It corresponds to the ordinal 0. The natural numbers are the finite trees with unary branchings

$$\Big|\; = 1 \qquad \Big|\; = 2 \qquad \Big|\; = 3$$

And so on through the natural numbers. The first infinite ordinal is the smallest tree that can be embedded in all finite trees except the unary ones. We have

And some other infinite ordinals

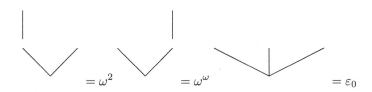

Let us now define the ordering. We start with finite trees — the root is downmost and the branching is ordered from left to right.

We write $\langle \mathbf{A} \rangle$ for the finite sequence of immediate subtrees of the tree $\mathbf{A}$, and $\langle \cdot \rangle$ is the empty sequence. Equality between trees is the usual equality. Given that we already know the ordering of some trees we let

$\mathbf{A} \leq \langle \mathbf{B} \rangle$: There is an immediate subtree $\mathbf{B}_i$ of $\mathbf{B}$ such that either $\mathbf{A} < \mathbf{B}_i$ or $\mathbf{A} = \mathbf{B}_i$

$\langle \mathbf{A} \rangle < \mathbf{B}$: For all immediate subtrees $\mathbf{A}_j$ of $\mathbf{A}$ we have $\mathbf{A}_j < \mathbf{B}$

$\langle \mathbf{A} \rangle < \langle \mathbf{B} \rangle$: The inverse lexicographical ordering of the immediate subtrees — we first check which sequence have smallest length, and if they have equal length we look at the rightmost immediate subtree where they differ

We define the ordering of trees by recursion over the immediate subtrees.

$$\mathbf{A} < \mathbf{B} \iff \mathbf{A} \leq \langle \mathbf{B} \rangle \ \lor \ (\langle \mathbf{A} \rangle < \mathbf{B} \land \langle \mathbf{A} \rangle < \langle \mathbf{B} \rangle)$$

All this is straightforward from a constructive point of view. It is a simple exercise to write a programs for deciding the ordering. Now to some simple properties proved by induction over heights of the trees

Transitivity $S < T$ and $T < U$ gives $S < U$

Irreflexivity For no S: $S < S$

Totality $S < T$ or $S = T$ or $T < S$ and these cases are mutually exclusive

Equality $S = T$ if they are equal as trees

We go through the proof that the ordering is transitive. So assume we have $S < T$ and $T < U$. We then prove by induction over the heights that $S < U$ and consider the following cases:

$\mathbf{T} \leq \langle \mathbf{U} \rangle$: By induction $S \leq \langle U \rangle$ and $S < U$

$\langle \mathbf{T} \rangle < \mathbf{U}$ **and** $\langle \mathbf{T} \rangle < \langle \mathbf{U} \rangle$: Consider the cases of $S < T$

$\qquad \mathbf{S} \leq \langle \mathbf{T} \rangle$: Using $S \leq \langle T \rangle < U$ we get by induction $S < U$

$\qquad \langle \mathbf{S} \rangle < \mathbf{T}$ **and** $\langle \mathbf{S} \rangle < \langle \mathbf{T} \rangle$: By induction we first get $\langle S \rangle < U$. Then from $\langle S \rangle < \langle T \rangle < \langle U \rangle$ we get $\langle S \rangle < \langle U \rangle$ and can conclude that $S < U$.

6.2 Deciding the ordering

There is more work to calculate the ordinals of the trees above.
We distinguish between properties which are given by ordinary
induction over the height of the trees and those properties where
we need more complicated methods of proofs. For the proofs it
may be worthwhile to look at a decision tree for the ordering:

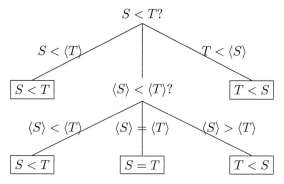

We start at the top and want to decide the ordering between
S and T. First we look at whether

- $S < \langle T \rangle$

- $T < \langle S \rangle$

In the first case we go to the left and conclude $S < T$. In the
second case we go to the right and conclude $T < S$. If neither we
proceed down the middle and look at the lexicographical order-
ing between $\langle S \rangle$ and $\langle T \rangle$ and from the three possible outcomes

we get $S < T$, $S = T$ or $T < S$. So to decide the ordering between S and T we only need to look at ordering between S or T and subtrees of them. This shows immediately that the ordering is decidable. Note that we get $S = T$ when the two trees are equal. It is a pleasant property that the equality in the ordering is simply ordinary equality of trees. Each ordinal which corresponds to a tree, corresponds to a unique tree. Below we shall often write down an ordinal instead of the corresponding tree.

6.3 Embeddings

We have an ordinary embedding of tree S into tree T whenever we have an injection of the nodes of S into the nodes of T respecting the treeordering. If we have an ordinary embedding we also get an injection of paths in S into paths in T. Now we are here not interested in the general notion of embeddings, but in the so called topological embedding. Then we require in addition of the injection of paths that the paths should not meet at interior nodes. An example will make it clearer. The tree

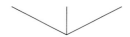

can be embedded into

We see that two of the paths will have an interior node in common. In fact the first tree cannot be topologically embedded into the second tree.

Let $\langle S \rangle = \langle S_i \rangle_{i \in I}$ and $\langle T \rangle = \langle T_j \rangle_{j \in J}$ be the immediate subtrees of S and T. We extend an ordering $\preceq$ to the immediate subtrees by writing $\langle S \rangle \preceq \langle T \rangle$ for there is an increasing function f from I into J with $S_i \preceq T_{fi}$. Using this we get the important properties of embeddings

- $\langle S \rangle \preceq \langle T \rangle \Rightarrow S \preceq T$

- $S \preceq \langle T \rangle \Rightarrow S \prec T$

Note that the empty tree is always $\preceq$ all other trees. We get monotonicity — if $S \preceq T$ then $\mathcal{F}(S) \preceq \mathcal{F}(T)$ where we get $\mathcal{F}(T)$ from $\mathcal{F}(S)$ by replacing an S with a T.

For topological embeddings we also have if the branching of S at the root is less than the branching of T

- $S \preceq \langle T \rangle \Leftrightarrow S \prec T$

By induction over the build up of trees

Theorem 6.1 (Embedding) *If S can be topologically embedded in T, then $S \leq T$.*

The first tree above corresponds to the ordinal ε_0 and the second one to ω^2 as we shall see. This shows that the first tree cannot be topologically embedded in the second.

Our ordering goes beyond topological embedding. The ordering is a linear order but the topological embedding is just a partial order. In particular the ordering has a left to right bias, while the topological embedding has no such bias.

The trees are nicely stratified. The smallest tree is the empty tree. Then comes the ones with unary branching. If a tree has one binary branch, then we can topologically embed

into it. So the tree is the smallest tree among the trees with at least one binary branch. Similar results for trees with one ternary branch, and so on.

6.4 Some calculations

So far we only know that each finite tree has an ordertype. In fact it turns out that the ordertypes are ordinals. We show this first by actually calculating the ordertypes. Later we shall show in a more direct way that the ordering is a well ordering.

The empty tree is the smallest tree and corresponds to the ordinal 0.

It is already some effort to show that we can define the successor function in a simple way. We have:

$$\overset{\alpha}{\underset{\cdot}{\mid}} = \alpha + 1$$

We do this by showing:

$$A < B \Leftrightarrow \overset{A}{\underset{\cdot}{\mid}} \leq B$$

or equivalently

$$B < \overset{A}{\underset{\cdot}{\mid}} \Leftrightarrow B \leq A$$

by induction over the heights. It is obviously true if one of the trees are empty. The one way of the equivalences follows from:

$$B \leq A < \overset{A}{\underset{\cdot}{\mid}}$$

So assume

$$B < \overset{A}{\underset{\cdot}{\mid}}$$

Then either B is empty — and we get $B \leq A$ and are done — or we get if the branching in B is unary:

$$B = \begin{array}{c} B_0 \\ \vdots \end{array}$$

But then by monotonicity:

$$B_0 < A$$

By induction:

$$B = \begin{array}{c} B_0 \\ \vdots \end{array} \leq A$$

If the branching in B is more than unary, then we must use the first clause in the definition of the ordering and we get immediately:

$$B \leq A$$

To get order types for other trees we show how we can build up the order types from below. Note that this is done by induction over the height of the trees.

Constructing trees

7.1 Building up from below

Given a tree $\mathbf{A}$ with immediate subtrees A_i

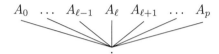

$$A_0 \quad \ldots \quad A_{\ell-1} \quad A_\ell \quad A_{\ell+1} \quad \ldots \quad A_p$$

The immediate subtrees A_i of $\mathbf{A}$ are smaller.
Now assume

- $B_l < A_l$

- $C_i < \mathbf{A}$ for all $i < l$

Then the following tree is less than $\mathbf{A}$

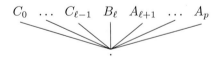

$$C_0 \quad \ldots \quad C_{\ell-1} \quad B_\ell \quad A_{\ell+1} \quad \ldots \quad A_p$$

This can be rephrased that for $b_l < a_l$ the function which to $x_0, \ldots, x_{\ell-1}$ gives

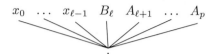

is closed under **A**. We also get that for $s < p$ that **A** is closed under the function which to $x_0, \ldots, x_s$ gives

This is interesting. Given a tree **A** we find both smaller trees and operations on trees which are closed under **A**

Fundamental subtrees of A : The immediate subtrees of **A**.

Fundamental functions of A : The two types of functions above.

Fundamental set of A : The set of trees generated by the fundamental functions starting with the fundamental subtrees.

Elementary fundamental function of A : We first get unary functions by letting all variables except the rightmost be 0. Then use all such unary functions of the first type. If there are no functions of the first type use the one of the second type with largest branching.

Elementary fundamental set of A : The set of trees generated by the elementary fundamental functions starting with the fundamental subtrees.

We denote the fundamental set of **A** with $\mathcal{F}(\mathbf{A})$ and we shall write it as

$$[S, \ldots, T | F, \ldots, G]$$

where we have displayed the fundamental subtrees $S, \ldots, T$ and the fundamental functions $F, \ldots, G$. Similarly for the elementary fundamental set $\mathcal{H}(\mathbf{A})$

We have the following:

$$\mathcal{F}(\,\cdot\,) \;=\; \emptyset$$

$$\mathcal{F}(\,\overset{\cdot}{\underset{\cdot}{|}}\,) \;=\; [\,\cdot\,\|\,]$$

$$\mathcal{F}(\,\overset{\cdot\ \ \cdot}{\bigvee}\,) \;=\; [\,\cdot\,|\,\overset{x}{\underset{\cdot}{|}}\,]$$

$$\mathcal{F}(\,\overset{\overset{|}{\bigvee}}{}\,) \;=\; [\,\cdot\,,\,\overset{\cdot}{\underset{\cdot}{|}}\,|\,\overset{x}{\underset{\cdot}{|}}\,,\,\overset{y\ \ \cdot}{\bigvee}\,]$$

$$\mathcal{F}(\,\bigvee\hspace{-1em}\bigvee\,) \;=\; [\,\cdot\,,\,\overset{\cdot}{\underset{\cdot}{|}}\,|\,\overset{x}{\underset{\cdot}{|}}\,,\,\overset{y\ \ z}{\bigvee}\,]$$

$$\mathcal{H}(\,\bigvee\hspace{-1em}\bigvee\,) \;=\; [\,\cdot\,|\,\overset{\ \ x}{\bigvee}\,]$$

Here x, y, z are variables used for describing fundamental functions.

Now we note that the fundamental sets give an approximation of trees from below. In fact we have for any tree **A**:

$$\mathbf{B} < \mathbf{A} \Leftrightarrow \exists \mathbf{C} \in \mathcal{F}(\mathbf{A}).\mathbf{C} \geq \mathbf{B}$$

We prove this by induction over the height of $\mathbf{B}$. It is trivial for height 0. So assume it proved for smaller heights than the height of $\mathbf{B}$. The direction $\Leftarrow$ is obvious. We assume $\mathbf{B} < \mathbf{A}$ and divide up into cases:

$\mathbf{B} \leq \langle \mathbf{A} \rangle$: But then $\mathbf{B}$ is less than or equal to one of the fundamental sub trees of $\mathbf{A}$.

$\langle \mathbf{B} \rangle < \mathbf{A} \wedge \langle \mathbf{B} \rangle < \langle \mathbf{A} \rangle$: By induction — to each immediate sub tree $\mathbf{B}_i$ there is an $\mathbf{C}_i \in \mathcal{F}(\mathbf{A})$ with $\mathbf{C}_i \geq \mathbf{B}_i$. Depending on how we prove $\langle \mathbf{B} \rangle < \langle \mathbf{A} \rangle$ we get a fundamental function which we can apply to some of the $\mathbf{C}_i$'s to get a $\mathbf{C} \in \mathcal{F}(\mathbf{A})$ with $\mathbf{C} \geq \mathbf{B}$

And it is proved. We can also use the elementary fundamental set

For any tree $\mathbf{A}$:

$$\mathbf{B} < \mathbf{A} \Leftrightarrow \exists \mathbf{C} \in \mathcal{H}(\mathbf{A}).\mathbf{C} \geq \mathbf{B}$$

We only need to note that

where $\gamma > \max(\alpha, \beta)$ and that the result of of an application of the second type of fundamental function can be embedded into an application of the first type.

With some extra assumption we can conclude that the fundamental set is not only an approximation from below, but that it contains all smaller trees. The extra assumption is that all trees less than or equal to the fundamental sub trees of $\mathbf{A}$ is contained in $\mathcal{F}(\mathbf{A})$. We then have

$$\mathbf{B} < \mathbf{A} \Leftrightarrow \mathbf{B} \in \mathcal{F}(\mathbf{A})$$

The proof follows the lines above. We have induction over the height of $\mathbf{B}$ and get to the cases

$\mathbf{B} \leq \langle \mathbf{A} \rangle$ **:** Then by assumption $\mathbf{B} \in \mathcal{F}(\mathbf{A})$.

$\langle \mathbf{B} \rangle < \mathbf{A} \wedge \langle \mathbf{B} \rangle < \langle \mathbf{A} \rangle$ **:** By induction — for each immediate sub tree $\mathbf{B}_i$ we have $\mathbf{B}_i \in \mathcal{F}(\mathbf{A})$. Depending on how we prove $\langle \mathbf{B} \rangle < \langle \mathbf{A} \rangle$ we get a fundamental function which we can apply to the $\mathbf{B}_i$'s to get $\mathbf{B} \in \mathcal{F}(\mathbf{A})$.

We are now getting a clearer picture of the ordering. The trees can be divided into layers — we let $\mathcal{T}_i$ be the trees with at most i-branchings. We then get that $\mathcal{T}_1$ is majorised by

and this tree is the least in $\mathcal{T} - \mathcal{T}_1$. The $\mathcal{T}_2$ is majorised by

and this tree is the least in $\mathcal{T} - \mathcal{T}_2$. The $\mathcal{T}_3$ are majorised by and this tree is the least in $\mathcal{T} - \mathcal{T}_3$. And so on.

7.2 Normal functions and ordinal notations

The geometrical way of characterizing ordinals gives us the ordinals up to ε_0 — but not much more. Oswald Veblen showed in 1908 how to get much further. So let us see how this can be done.

A unary function F of ordinals into ordinals is *normal* if both

Strictly monotone increasing: $\alpha < \beta \Rightarrow F\alpha < F\beta$

Continuous: For an increasing sequence α_i we have $F \sup \alpha_i = \sup F\alpha_i$

The main property about normal functions is that they have fix points. Given an ordinal α the first fix points above α is given as the limit of

$$\alpha, F\alpha, FF\alpha, FFF\alpha, \ldots$$

If we have a countable family $\mathcal{F}$ of normal functions, we can find a common fix point by applying the functions from $\mathcal{F}$ in a fair way. The fix points is a closed unbounded set of ordinals. Conversely if we have a closed and unbounded set of ordinals its enumerating function is normal. A normal function F is increasing — $x \leq Fx$. (For assume not and let α be the smallest ordinal with $F\alpha < \alpha$. But then $FF\alpha < F\alpha < \alpha$ and we have found an even smaller ordinal.)

Since Veblens paper from 1908 we know how to build a hierarchy of normal functions. There are two operations

Unary to binary: Given a normal function Fx. The binary function Fxy of ordinals which is normal in x and strictly monotone increasing in y is given by

- $Fx0 = Fx$

- $Fxy = $ the x'th common fix point of $\lambda u.Fuz$ for all $z < y$

Diagonalization: Given a binary function Fxy as constructed from a normal function F as above. We define a unary function $Gy = F0y$. This unary function is seen to be normal.

We now start with a unary normal function F and build a hierarchy of n-ary functions above it. We describe how it is done for quaternary functions and leave the general construction to the reader.

- $Fx0 = Fx$

- $Fxy0 = Fxy$

- $Fxyz0 = Fxyz$

$y > 0$: $Fxyzu =$ the x'th common fix point of $\lambda v.Fvy'zu$ for all $y' < y$

$z > 0$: $F0yzu =$ the y'th common fix point of $\lambda v.F0vz'u$ for all $z' < z$

$u > 0$: $F00zu =$ the z'th common fix point of $\lambda v.F00vu'$ for all $u' < u$

There are no binary function of ordinal which is normal in one argument and strictly monotone increasing in the other. For assume $F\alpha\beta$ is such a binary function which is normal in the first argument. Let β_1 and β_2 be given. Then the functions $\lambda x.Fx\beta_1$ and $\lambda x.Fx\beta_2$ have a common fix point Y and hence $FY\beta_1 = Y = FY\beta_2$ and since F is increasing in the second argument we get $\beta_1 = \beta_2$ and the function is not strictly monotone increasing in the second argument.

In this way we get a system of notations for ordinals. It is common to start with the normal function $\lambda x.\omega^x$. We write this as ϕx. Then we have

- ε_0 is the first fix point. $\varepsilon_0 = \phi 01$

- Γ_0 is the first fix point of the diagonalization of the binary functions. $\Gamma_0 = \phi 001$

- The small Veblen ordinal is the supremum of the ordinals described by this hierarchy

Observe that we define the n-ary functions by just looking at a couple of the arguments. We can extend the hierarchy to functions with an infinite number of arguments — the arguments ordered by ordinals and only a finite number of them different from 0. If we do this we get ordinal notations up to the socalled large Veblen ordinal and a notation system for it is given by Kurt Schüttes Klammersymbole.

Later when we come to the order type of finite trees we need to consider a variant of the normal functions. Let F be a normal function. We then have defined

- The range of F: R_F

- The fix points of F: FIX_F

We let F^* be the function enumerating $R_F - \text{FIX}_F$. So $F*$ is like F except that it jumps over fix points. We write

$$F^* \sim F$$

where F is a normal function and F^* is the same as F except that it jumps over fix points.

7.3 Further calculations

We have shown that the empty tree has order type 0 and that

$$\cdot \; = 0 \qquad\qquad \overset{\displaystyle \alpha}{\big|} \; = \alpha + 1$$

We now try to characterize the function

But this is the supremum of the set of α closed under the successor function. The function $\omega \cdot x$ enumerates the limit points. Now we observe that we therefore have after calibrating the start and observing that we jump over fix points

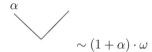

$$\sim (1 + \alpha) \cdot \omega$$

Now to the function

For $\alpha = 0$ it is ω. For $\alpha > 0$ it is the supremum of the ordinals starting with α and closed under all

where $\alpha-$ runs over ordinals $< \alpha$. This gives for $\alpha < \epsilon_0$

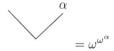

$$= \omega^{\omega^\alpha}$$

At ε_0 we have a fix point of the function ω^{ω^α}. In the tree function we jump over the fix point and get

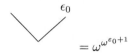

For the full function we write

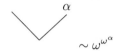

where the $\sim$ indicates that we jump over the fix points. We can then go on

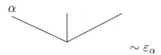

where ε_α is the enumerating function of the ε-numbers. The critical ε-numbers are the numbers κ with $\varepsilon_\kappa = \kappa$. Let κ_α be the function enumerating them. Then

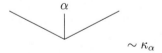

The ordinal Γ_0 is the first fix point of the enumeration κ_α of the critical ε-numbers. We have:

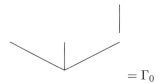 $= \Gamma_0$

Too sum up

- We prove by direct calculation that the order types of the finite trees are in fact ordinals. Later we shall give other proofs of it.

- The tree functions correspond in a direct way to the Veblen hierarchy of functions where we jump over the fix points.

- The limit of the order type of the finite trees is the small Veblen ordinal.

Now let us introduce some new notation instead of the trees

$$\Psi(\alpha) =$$

$$\Psi(\alpha, \beta) =$$

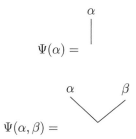

$$\Psi(\alpha, \beta, \gamma) =$$

And so on. Let us write

$$\Psi_k(\alpha, \beta, \ldots) = \Psi(0, \ldots, 0, \alpha, \beta, \ldots)$$

where we have 0's in the first k arguments. And we write

$$\Psi_k^n(\alpha, \beta, \ldots),$$

for n times iteration of $\lambda x . \Psi_k(x, \beta, \ldots)$ starting with α. We use this in describing the effect of elementary fundamental sets. With this notation we can sum up what can be proved here in Skolem arithmetic

- $\alpha < \Psi(\beta) \leftrightarrow \alpha \leq \beta$

- $\alpha < \Psi(\beta, 0) \leftrightarrow \exists n . \alpha \leq \Psi_0^n(\beta)$

- For $\beta > 0$: $\alpha < \Psi(0, \beta) \leftrightarrow \exists n . \alpha \leq \Psi_0^n(\beta, \beta-)$ for some $\beta- < \beta$

- $\alpha < \Psi(0, 0, 0) \leftrightarrow \exists n . \alpha \leq \Psi_1^n(0)$

- For $\beta > 0$: $\alpha < \Psi(\beta, 0, 0) \leftrightarrow \exists n . \alpha \leq \Psi_1^n(\Psi(\beta-, 0, 0))$ for some $\beta- < \beta$

- For $\beta > 0$: $\alpha < \Psi(0, \beta, 0) \leftrightarrow \exists n . \alpha \leq \Psi_0^n(\beta, \beta-, 0)$ for some $\beta- < \beta$

- For $\beta > 0$: $\alpha < \Psi(0, 0, \beta) \leftrightarrow \exists n.\alpha \leq \Psi_1^n(\beta, \beta-)$ for some $\beta- < \beta$

- $\alpha < \Psi(0, 0, 0, 0) \leftrightarrow \exists n.\alpha \leq \Psi_2^n(0)$

- And so on

7.4 Proof of wellordering

So far we have only used ordinary quantifier free induction over the heights of trees to prove properties, but more is needed to prove that the tree ordering is well founded. We give three proofs.

Using Kruskals theorem:

Kruskals theorem says that if we have an infinite sequence of finite trees $T_0, T_1, \ldots$, then there are numbers $m < n$ such that T_m is topologically embedded in T_n. But then $T_m < T_n$ and no infinite sequence of finite trees can be infinitely descending.

Using inductive definitions:

We prove that if $\mathbf{T}_1, \ldots, \mathbf{T}_n$ are well founded then so is also all $\mathbf{A}$ with

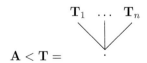

$$\mathbf{A} < \mathbf{T} =$$

and hence $\mathbf{T}$ itself is well founded. This is done by induction over

- the height of $\mathbf{A}$

- the sequence $\mathbf{T}_1, \ldots, \mathbf{T}_n$ ordered by the inverse lexicographical ordering of tree ordering

So assume we have $\mathbf{T}_1, \ldots, \mathbf{T}_n$ well founded and $\mathbf{A} < \mathbf{T}$. We then have the following cases

$\mathbf{A} \leq \langle \mathbf{T} \rangle$: Then $\mathbf{A} \leq \mathbf{T}_i$ for some i and is therefore well founded.

$\langle \mathbf{A} \rangle < \mathbf{T} \wedge \langle \mathbf{A} \rangle < \langle \mathbf{T} \rangle$: Then all immediate subtrees of $\mathbf{A}$ are less than $\mathbf{T}$ and by induction over height of $\mathbf{A}$ the immediate subtrees of $\mathbf{A}$ are well founded. But the immediate subtrees of $\mathbf{A}$ comes before the immediate subtrees of $\mathbf{T}$ in the inverse lexicographical ordering. We conclude that $\mathbf{A}$ is well founded.

We then get that all finite trees are well founded by some giant — and perhaps not so informative — step.

Using minimal bad sequence:

A bad sequence is an infinitely descending sequence $A_0, A_1, A_2, A_3,$ It is minimal bad if

- A_0 is of minimal height starting an infinite descending sequence with A_0

- A_1 is of minimal height starting an infinite descending sequence with A_0, A_1

- A_2 is of minimal height starting an infinite descending sequence with A_0, A_1, A_2

- and so on

Given a bad sequence we can find a minimal bad sequence. In such a minimal bad sequence none of the immediate sub trees of the elements are bad. Now assume we have a bad sequence and hence a minimal bad sequence $A_0, A_1, A_2, \ldots$. Then by minimality we can only use the second condition in the definition of the ordering

$$A_i > A_{i+1} \Leftrightarrow \langle A_i \rangle \geq A_{i+1} \vee (A_i > \langle A_{i+1} \rangle \wedge \langle A_i \rangle > \langle A_{i+1} \rangle)$$

Therefore we have a descending sequence in the lexicographical ordering

$$\langle A_0 \rangle > \langle A_1 \rangle > \langle A_2 \rangle > \langle A_3 \rangle > \cdots$$

Then after a while these sequences must have the same length and we can find an element in one of them which is bad. So we have an immediate sub tree of one of the elements which is bad — contradicting the minimality of the original sequence. Therefore there are no bad sequences and the ordering is a well ordering.

Combinatorics

8

We started proof theory by first developing natural numbers as a data structure. We developed logical systems for describing them. But found that we had to use ordinals in the analysis of the systems. The ordinals could be seen as coming from the data structure of finite trees and where we have a special ordering between the trees. In this chapter we shall investigate this.

8.1 Ramseys theorem

Ramseys theorem can be seen as a generalization of the pigeon hole principle. We treat it here as a preparation for Higmans lemma and Kruskals theorem where we come closer to the tree properties which we have used.

Theorem 8.1 (Ramsey) *We start with an infinite set A, a finite set of colors C and a coloring of all pairs of elements i.e. a function $\phi : A^{(2)} \to C$. Then there is an infinite subset $B \subset A$ such that all pairs from B are colored with the same color.*

The pairs are unordered with distinct elements. We do not count (x, y) as different from (y, x) and we have $x \neq y$.

We give Skolems proof of the Ramsey theorem. The following picture gives the idea

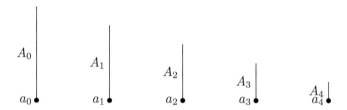

- We start with the infinite set $A_0 = A$

- Pick an element a_0 from A_0

- We consider the colors of the pairs with a_0 and another element from A_0

- One of the colors, c_0, is repeated infinitely many times

- Let A_1 be an infinite subset of A_0 with elements b such that (a_0, b) are colored with c_0. Pick element a_1 from A_1.

- Repeat the above with the infinite set A_1 and a_1 to get c_1, A_2 and a_2 — and so on

- For each a_i all elements b to the right are such that (a_i, b) are colored with c_i

- One of the colors c_j is repeated infinitely often with corresponding points a_{j_i}

- The infinite set $a_{j_0}, a_{j_1}, a_{j_2}, \ldots$ is the sought subset B of A with all pairs colored with c_j

The same idea can be used to give other versions of Ramsey theorem

Higher order tuples: Given the Ramsey theorem for pairs we can use the same argument to give the theorem for triples. We then let c_0 and A_1 be such that all for all pairs b, c from A_1 the triples (a_0, b, c) is given color c_0. The infinite subset A_1 of A_0 is given by the Ramsey theorem for pairs. Then follow the rest of the argument above. Similarly for n-tuples.

Finite version: Given the wanted size of the monochromatic set and the number of colors, we can work backwards to find how large the original set could be to guarantee the size of a monochromatic set no matter how the coloring is.

8.2 Kruskals theorem

We consider the following ordering relations

Quasi order: Transitive and reflexive

Partial order: Quasi order which is also antisymmetric

Linear order: Partial order which is also total

And on these we have wellfoundedness properties

Well quasi order (WQO): Quasi order such that to every infinite sequence $a_0, a_1, a_2, \ldots$ there are $i < j$ with $a_i \leq a_j$

Well partial order (WPO): Well quasi order which is a partial order

Well order (WO): Well quasi order which is a linear order

The following is equivalent to being a well quasi order

- To every infinite sequence there is an infinite ascending subsequence $a_{i_0} \leq a_{i_1} \leq a_{i_2} \leq \cdots$

- There are no infinite strictly descending sequence and no infinite set of pairwise incomparable elements

Let us prove the first equivalence. So assume we have a well quasi order and an infinite sequence $a_0, a_1, a_2, \ldots$. We then give a coloring of the pairs (a_i, a_j) with $i < j$ by mapping it to $\leq, >, |$ depending on the order relation between a_i and a_j. By Ramsey theorem we have an infinite monochromatic subset. This must be the sought infinite ascending subsequence. The other way is trivial.

We have the following operations on orderings

Products: The product $A \times B$ is given by taking the ordering of each coordinate separately

Strings: The set of finite strings over A, $A^\star$, is ordered by letting $(a_0, \ldots, a_{m-1}) \leq (b_0, \ldots, b_{n-1})$ if there is a monotone strictly increasing $f : m \to n$ with $a_{f_i} \leq b_i$ for all $i < m$

We then have

Theorem 8.2 *The product of two WQO's is again WQO*

We call a pair of elements (a, b) in an ordering for good if $a \leq b$. A sequence $a_0, a_1, \ldots$ of elements is good if it contains a good pair ($a_i \leq a_j$ for $i < j$). Else it is bad. So we have a WQO if every infinite sequence is good. Above we proved that if we have an infinite sequence in a WQO, we can find an infinite subsequence where all pairs are good.

Now assume A and B are WQO. Let $(a_0, b_0), (a_1, b_1), \ldots$ be an infinite sequence. Then the infinite sequence $a_0, a_1, \ldots$ have an infinite subsequence $a_{i_0}, a_{i_1}, a_{i_2}, \ldots$ where all the pairs are good. Then the infinite sequence in B, $b_{i_0}, b_{i_1}, b_{i_2}, \ldots$ have a good pair b_{i_m}, b_{i_n} and the pair $(a_{i_m}, b_{i_m}), (a_{i_n}, b_{i_n})$ is good in $A \times B$ and $A \times B$ is a WQO.

Theorem 8.3 (Higmans lemma) *The finite strings over a WQO is again a WQO*

Let A be a WQO and $A * \star$ the quasi ordering of finite strings. Assume we have an infinite bad sequence. We construct an infinite minimal bad sequence $\alpha_0, \alpha_1, \alpha_2, \ldots$ — minimal as follows

- α_0 is of minimal length such that we have an infinite bad sequence starting with α_0

- α_1 is of minimal length such that we have an infinite bad sequence starting with α_0, α_1

- α_2 is of minimal length such that we have an infinite bad sequence starting with $\alpha_0, \alpha_1, \alpha_2$ — and so on

We first observe that none of the elements in the sequence are empty. So we can write the sequence as

$$(a_0, \beta_0), (a_1, \beta_0), (a_2, \beta_2), \ldots$$

Let $B^\star$ be the set of $\beta_0, \beta_1, \beta_2, \ldots$. It is a subset of $A^\star$ and hence a quasi ordering. We show that it is a WQO. Assume we have an infinite sequence starting with say β_i. If this sequence involves an infinite number of times the β_k with $k < i$, then we immediately get a good pair. Else we can assume that the sequence only involves β_k with $k \geq i$. Consider now the sequence

$$\alpha_0, \alpha_1, \ldots, \alpha_{i-1}, \beta_i, \beta'_{i+1}, \beta'_{i+2}, \ldots$$

By minimality of α_i there must be a good pair. This good pair cannot involve any of the α's — neither as α_k, α_l nor as α_k, β_m. In the last case we would get $\alpha_k \leq \beta_m \leq \alpha_m$. So we must have a good pair among the β's. Therefore $B^\star$ is a WQO. Furthermore $A \times B^\star$ is a WQO and we have a contradiction.

Theorem 8.4 (Kruskal) *The finite trees ordered by topological embedding is a WQO*

Let $\mathcal{T}$ be the set of finite trees ordered by topological embedding. Each such tree T can be considered as a sequence of its immediate subtrees. Assume we have a bad sequence of finite trees. As above we construct a minimal bad sequence, $T_0, T_1, \ldots$ of trees where the minimality is by the height of the trees. Let the set of all immediate subtrees in the sequence be $\mathcal{F}$. We show that $\mathcal{F}$ is a WQO. Assume we have an infinite sequence $S_k, S_{k+1}, S_{k+2}, \ldots$ from $\mathcal{F}$ where S_k is an immediate subtree of T_k. If there is an infinite number of elements from the sequence involving immediate subtrees of T_i where $i < k$, then we immediately get a good pair. Else we can assume that the infinite sequence only involves immediate subtrees of the trees T_i where $i \geq k$. Consider now the sequence

$$T_0, T_1, \ldots, T_{k-1}, S_k, S_{k+1}, \ldots$$

By minimality of T_k it must have a good pair. This good pair cannot involve the T's — neither as T_i, T_j nor as T_i, S_j. So it must have a good pair among the S's and we get that $\mathcal{F}$ is a WQO. By Higmans lemma we get that the sequences $\mathcal{F}*$ is also a WQO and hence so is $\mathcal{T}$.

The statement of Kruskals theorem involves topological embeddings. It is also true for embeddings, but the topological embedding formulation is stronger and it is reflected in the proof. We build our embeddings by using embeddings of the immediate subtrees and then glueing them together at the root.

8.3 Linearization

A quasi order $\leq$ can always be extended to a linear order. Assume that we have an order $\leq$ and an incomparable pair of elements $a|b$. We extend $\leq$ to $\leq^*$ where $a \leq^* b$ by defining

$$c \leq^* d \Leftrightarrow c \leq d \vee (c \leq a \wedge b \leq d)$$

Using the incomparability $a|b$ we get

- $\leq^*$ is transitive

- $\leq^*$ is antisymmetric if $\leq$ is

For transitivity assume $c \leq^* d \leq^* e$. Between c and e we have a chain of $\leq$ interspersed with $a \leq^* b$. Observe that we can have at most one such pair. Assume we had two. Use transitivity of $\leq$ to shorten the chain. Then we get $a \leq^* b \leq a \leq^* b$ which contradicts the incomparability $a|b$. And $c \leq^* e$. For the antisymmetry assume we have $c \leq a \leq^* b \leq c$. Then $b \leq a$ contradicting incomparability. So there are no other $\leq^*$-chains from c to c than those which are also $\leq$-chains.

The ordering $\leq^*$ is the minimal one extending $\leq$ and having a less than b. The obstructions to such an extensions are the set of incomparable pairs. We can force any of these to be ordered in the one or the other way. After having done it as above, some of the old incomparable pairs may be comparable, but none of the comparable pairs become incomparable. We get

- Every partial order can be extended to a linear order

- A well partial order is a partial order where every linear extension is a well order

Given a set $\mathcal{S}$ of finite trees. They are partially ordered by topological embedding. For an $S \in \mathcal{S}$ it is given different order type using the different linear extensions of the topological embedding in $\mathcal{S}$. We have already met one linear extension — the one given by inverse lexicographical ordering of the immediate subtrees. By ordering the branchings some other way we may get another linear extension. The two trees below

 and

are incomparable in the topological embedding and in the linear extensions we are free how to order them. For a finite tree T we define $T^\dagger$ to be the maximal tree in our tree ordering obtained from T by permuting the branches. Now we want to compare for $S \in \mathcal{S}$ with respect to our tree ordering

$|S|$: The supremum of order types of S in linear extensions

$S^\dagger$: the maximal tree in our tree ordering obtained from S by permuting the branches

Theorem 8.5
$$|S| \leq S^\dagger$$

This is proved by induction on the height of the trees. Note

- the proof uses only simple induction — it can be done in Skolem arithmetic

- the calculation of $S^\dagger$ from S is also done in Skolem arithmetic

- the well ordering of our tree ordering shows that the topological embedding is WQO — it gives a new proof of Kruskals theorem

8.4 Transfinite induction

We assume that we have some way of representing ordinals, and then define transfinite induction for some formula F up to some ordinal α by

$$\mathbf{PROG}(F) \quad : \quad \forall\beta(\forall\gamma < \beta F(\gamma) \to F(\beta))$$
$$\mathbf{TI}(\alpha, F) \quad : \quad \mathbf{PROG}(F) \to \forall\beta < \alpha F(\beta)$$
$$\mathbf{TI}(\alpha) \quad : \quad \mathbf{TI}(\alpha, F) \text{ for all formulas } F$$

First observe that transfinite induction behaves nicely with respect to inequality

$$\mathbf{TI}(\beta) \wedge \alpha < \beta \to \mathbf{TI}(\alpha)$$

Then we go through the build-up of the finite trees. We have

$$\mathbf{TI}(0, F)$$

This is trivially true. We have $\forall x < 0.Gx$ for any formula Gx.

$$\mathbf{TI}(\alpha, F) \to \mathbf{TI}(\Psi(\alpha), F)$$

So assume $\mathbf{TI}(\alpha, F)$ and $\mathbf{PROG}(F)$. We then get $\forall x < \alpha.Fx$. From $\mathbf{PROG}(F)$ we also get $\forall x \leq \alpha.Fx$. But then $\forall x < \Psi(\alpha).Fx$ since $x < \Psi(\alpha) \leftrightarrow x \leq \alpha$ as we have previously proved.

Now to the next step we prove a similar statement

$$\mathbf{TI}(\alpha, F) \to \mathbf{TI}(\Psi(\alpha, 0), F)$$

Assume $\mathbf{PROG}(F)$ and $\mathbf{TI}(\alpha, F)$. We can prove in Skolem arithmetic

- $F\Psi_0^0(\alpha)$

- $F\Psi_0^n(\alpha) \to F\Psi_0^{n+1}(\alpha)$

Hence by quantifier free induction $F\Psi_0^n(\alpha)$ for all n, and $\mathbf{PROG}(F)$ gives $F\Psi(\alpha, 0)$ which should be proved.

Now we come to the next step. Here we no longer have the uniformity in the induction formula. Given formula F we find a formula F^* such that

$$\mathbf{TI}(\alpha, F^*) \to \mathbf{TI}(\Psi(0, \alpha), F)$$

Now observe that $\Psi(0, \alpha)$ is built up from below by $\Psi_0^n(\alpha, \alpha-)$ where $\alpha- < \alpha$. We define F^* so that it takes $\Psi_0^n(\alpha, \alpha-)$ steps instead of the small steps that F takes. We let

$$F^*\alpha = \forall x.(\forall z < x.Fz \to \forall z < \Psi_0(x, \alpha).Fz)$$

Given $F^*\beta$, we then have for each natural number n

$$\forall x.(\forall z < x.Fz \to \forall z < \Psi_0^n(x, \beta).Fz)$$

And by induction over the quantifier formula we get

$$\forall n.\forall x.(\forall z < x.Fz \to \forall z < \Psi_0^n(x, \beta).Fz)$$

These are the key steps in the proof. Now to the details. We first prove

$$\mathbf{Prog}(F) \rightarrow \mathbf{PROG}(F^*)$$

Let α be given and assume

- $\mathbf{PROG}(F)$

- $\forall y < \alpha.F^*y$

- $\alpha- < \alpha$

- An x

We then prove $\forall n.\forall z < \Psi_0^n(x, \alpha-).Fz$. And furthermore $\forall z < \Psi(x, \alpha).Fz$ which gives $\mathbf{PROG}(F^*)$. Now assume $\mathbf{PROG}(F)$ and $\mathbf{TI}(\alpha)$. Then $\mathbf{PROG}(F^*)$ and $\mathbf{TI}(\alpha, F^*)$ which gives

$$\forall x.(\forall z < x.Fz \rightarrow \forall z < \Psi(x, \alpha).Fz)$$

and inserting $x = 0$ gives

$$\forall z < \Psi(0, \alpha).Fz$$

and using $\mathbf{PROG}(F)$ we get $F\Psi(0, \alpha)$ as desired.

We can also see what is the obstruction to proving $\mathbf{TI}(\Psi(0, 0, 0)$ — or $\mathbf{TI}(\epsilon_0)$. Let us say that we want to prove $\mathbf{TI}(\Psi(0, 0, 0), F)$ for a Π_m^0 formula F. We must prove $\mathbf{TI}(\Psi_0^n(0, 0), F)$. But this proof depends on an ordinary induction over a Π_{m+n}^0-formula — and the proof is different for different n. It is no longer uniform. This is where Peano arithmetic is no longer able to prove what is true.

Labeled trees

9

9.1 Extending finite trees

We now extend our ordinal notations using labels on the nodes of finite trees. The labels are from a well ordered set Λ. In addition we have an extra label ∞ which is larger than all the labels from Λ. The labels $\Lambda = \{0\}$ correspond to our finite trees, but for larger Λ our orderings will not be any longer monotone and the orderings go far beyond what we have used so far.

So we have given a well ordered set Λ and the extra label ∞. They are well ordered by $<$. The plan now is to introduce for each $j \in \Lambda \cup \{\infty\}$ the following in a finite labeled tree T

- the sequence $\langle T \rangle_j$ of j-subtrees of T

- an ordering $<_j$ for each j

- the ordering $<_0$ is the one we shall use to compare trees

So first we define the j-subtrees. For $j = \infty$ we get the immediate subtrees as defined for finite trees. We have

$$\langle T \rangle_\infty = \langle T \rangle$$

Consider now a $j \in \Lambda$. A subtree S of T is a j-subtree if

- the root node in S have label j

- all nodes between the root of T and the root of S have labels $> j$ — the dashed line below

111

- there is no restriction on the label of the root node of T

The sequence of j-subtrees is denoted by

$$\langle T \rangle_j$$

We can now define the orderings of trees

$$S <_j T \Leftrightarrow S \leq_j \langle T \rangle_j \vee (\langle S \rangle_j <_j T \wedge S <_{j+} T)$$
$$S <_\infty T \Leftrightarrow \textit{lexicographical ordering}$$

Here we use abbreviations like for the finite trees

- $\leq_j$ means either ordinary $=$ or $<_j$

- $S \leq_j \langle T \rangle_j$: There exists a j-subtree T_0 of T with $S \leq_j T$

- $\langle S \rangle_j < T$: For all j-subtrees S_0 of S , $S_0 <_j T$

- $j+$ is the smallest label in S and T larger than j if it exists, else it is ∞

- The lexicographical ordering is such that we compare in priority

- The labels at the root of S and the root of T
- For the same label i: The lengths of $\langle S \rangle_i$ and $\langle T \rangle_i$
- The rightmost place where the two sequences differ in the $>_i$-ordering

Observe that if j does not occur in S, then S does not have any j-subtree and $\langle S \rangle_j$ is empty and conditions like $\langle S \rangle_j <_j T$ are trivially true and $T \leq_j \langle S \rangle_j$ are trivially false.

The relations $<_j$ are well defined. We define a relations by using either smaller trees or higher labels (among the finite number of them in the trees we compare).

We now show that the relations are all transitive. So assume we have

$$\mathbf{A} <_j \mathbf{B} <_j \mathbf{C}$$

and want to prove by induction that we get $\mathbf{A} <_j \mathbf{C}$. The induction uses either smaller trees or higher labels. First for $j \in \Lambda$

- $\mathbf{B} \leq_j \langle \mathbf{C} \rangle_j$: Then $\mathbf{A} <_j \mathbf{B} \leq_j \langle \mathbf{C} \rangle_j$, and by induction $\mathbf{A} \leq_j \langle \mathbf{C} \rangle_j$ and $\mathbf{A} <_j \mathbf{C}$

- $\mathbf{B} <_{j+} \mathbf{C}$ and $\langle \mathbf{B} \rangle_j <_j \mathbf{C}$: Then

  - $\mathbf{A} \leq_j \langle \mathbf{B} \rangle_j$: Then $\mathbf{A} \leq_j \langle \mathbf{B} \rangle_j <_j \mathbf{C}$ and by induction $\mathbf{A} <_j \mathbf{C}$

  - $\mathbf{A} <_{j+} \mathbf{B}$ and $\langle \mathbf{A} \rangle_j <_j \mathbf{B}$: Then we have $\mathbf{A} <_j \mathbf{C}$ from

* $\mathbf{A} <_{j+} \mathbf{B} <_{j+} \mathbf{C}$ which gives by induction $\mathbf{A} <_{j+} \mathbf{C}$

* $\langle \mathbf{A} \rangle_j <_j \mathbf{B} <_j \mathbf{C}$ which gives by induction $\langle \mathbf{A} \rangle_j <_j \mathbf{C}$

Then for $j = \infty$. Here we have

- The labels at (least two of) the roots are different. Then $\mathbf{A} <_\infty \mathbf{C}$

- The labels are the same. Then we compare immediate subtrees and by induction $\mathbf{A} <_\infty \mathbf{C}$

So the orderings are transitive. They are also total. We decide the ordering by a similar decision tree as for finite trees. To compare $\mathbf{A}$ and $\mathbf{B}$ we go through a number of tests and sequentially compare

- $A \leq_j \langle B \rangle_j$ — giving $A <_j B$

- $B \leq_j \langle A \rangle_j$ — giving $B <_j A$

- $A \leq_{j+} \langle B \rangle_{j+}$ — giving $A <_j B$

- $B \leq_{j+} \langle A \rangle_{j+}$ — giving $B <_j A$

- $A \leq_{j++} \langle B \rangle_{j++}$ — giving $A <_j B$

- $B \leq_{j++} \langle A \rangle_{j++}$ — giving $B <_j A$

- ...

- ...

- The root of A is less than the root of B — giving $A <_j B$

- The root of B is less than the root of A — giving $A <_j B$

- The roots have the same label i

- $\langle A \rangle <_i \langle B \rangle$ — giving $A <_j B$

- $\langle B \rangle <_i \langle A \rangle$ — giving $B <_j A$

- At last the roots must be the same and all immediate subtrees are the same — giving $A = B$

The test is read as follows: We start with line 1. If it succeds we are finished. Else we go to line 2. If it succeeds then we are finished. In this way we go through the tests line for line until we find a test which succeeds. If none succeds the two labeled trees must be equal.

In the finite labeled trees we do not just take immediate subtrees, we take j-subtrees for any label j. We have the following situation:

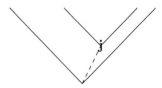

- no restriction on the label at the root

- the labels on the dashed line $> j$

So to get to the j-subtrees we first pass over the downmost node and then pass over all nodes $> j$ until we come to a node with label j. This gives a layered structure for the j-subtrees. Furthest above the root are the 0-subtrees. Then come the 1-subtrees, the 2-subtrees and so on. To get to the j subtrees we would never pass through the i subtrees for $i < j$. And if we look at the j-subtrees and then the j-subtrees of those, the j-subtrees of those and so on we would never go through the i-subtrees where $i < j$.

9.2   Well ordering of finite labeled trees

The proof follows Gaisi Takeutis proof that the ordinal diagrams are well ordered. We start with assuming that we have an infinite $<_0$-descending sequence of trees.

$$T_0 >_0 T_1 >_0 T_2 >_0 \ldots$$

Then we construct for each label i an infinite $<_i$-descending sequence satisfying some extra conditions. If we now look at the descending sequence for $i = \infty$ we get a contradiction. Instead of going directly through the whole construction, we start with the case where the only label in the trees is 0. This is the same as looking at finite trees. We start with constructing from the T_n's a minimal bad sequence

$$T_0^0 >_0 T_1^0 >_0 T_2^0 >_0 \ldots$$

A bad tree is one which is not well founded — there is an infinite $<_0$-descending sequence starting with it. A tree is minimal bad if it is bad but all of its immediate subtrees are not bad. Let us see how we construct a minimal bad tree from T_0. T_0 is bad but may not be minimal. If not then one of its immediate subtrees are bad. If this is not minimal, then we go to one of its immediate subtrees and so on. The topmost subtrees are not minimal bad. But either T_0 itself or one of its subtrees must be. Having now constructed a minimal bad sequence

$$T_0^0 >_0 T_1^0 >_0 \ldots >_0 T_n^0$$

we must show how to extend it. By construction T_n^0 is minimal bad and can be continued

$$T_0^0 >_0 T_1^0 >_0 \ldots >_0 T_n^0 >_0 S_{n+1} >_0 S_{n+2} >_0 \ldots$$

but where S_{n+1} is bad but may not be minimal. But then by the same construction above we have a subtree U_{n+1} which is minimal bad. Now observe that $T_n^0 >_0 U_{n+1}$ since U_{n+1} is just a subtree of S_{n+1}.

In this construction observe

- we must decide whether certain trees are bad or not — i.e. a Π_1^1-notion

- in the first place where the original bad sequence and the constructed minimal bad sequence differ, the one tree is a subtree of the other

Now we go to the definition of the ordering

$$\boxed{S <_j T \Leftrightarrow S \leq_j \langle T \rangle_j \vee (\langle S \rangle_j <_j T \wedge S <_{j+} T)}$$

Observe that the minimal badness excludes the first disjunct

$$\langle T_n^0 \rangle \geq_0 T_{n+1}^0$$

For then we would have an immediate subtree of T_n^0 which is bad. In our case $0+ = \infty$. Therefore we have

$$T_0^0 >_\infty T_1^0 >_\infty T_2^0 >_\infty \ldots$$

Then from some stage in the sequence

- all trees have equally many immediate subtrees

- there is a number k such that immediate subtree k is the rightmost place where they all differ and this immediate subtree must be bad

And this contradicts that all the trees in the sequence where minimal.

We now go to the general case. There are some changes. We assume there is a bad sequence and construct a minimal bad sequence. The badness (and goodness) refers to the $<_i$-orderings, but the minimality is more complicated. We define a tree T to be *i*-**good:** No infinitely descending $<_i$-sequence

i-**minimal:** For every $j \leq i$ all elements of $\langle T \rangle_j$ are j-good

The proof starts with assuming we have a $<_0$-bad sequence. We construct an array of i-minimal i-bad sequences

$$
\begin{array}{cccccccccccc}
T_0^0 & >_0 & T_1^0 & >_0 & T_2^0 & >_0 & T_3^0 & >_0 & T_4^0 & >_0 & \cdots \\
T_0^1 & >_1 & T_1^1 & >_1 & T_2^1 & >_1 & T_3^1 & >_1 & T_4^1 & >_1 & \cdots \\
T_0^2 & >_2 & T_1^2 & >_2 & T_2^2 & >_2 & T_3^2 & >_2 & T_4^2 & >_2 & \cdots \\
T_0^3 & >_3 & T_1^3 & >_3 & T_2^3 & >_3 & T_3^3 & >_3 & T_4^3 & >_3 & \cdots \\
\cdots & & \cdots & & \cdots & & \cdots & & \cdots & & \cdots
\end{array}
$$

First we show how to proceed at successor stages — from row i to row $i + 1$. So assume we have an i-bad and i-minimal sequence

$$T_0^i >_i T_1^i >_i T_2^i >_i \cdots$$

By i-minimality we cannot have $\langle T_i^k \rangle_i \geq_i T_i^{k+1}$ for any k. Hence

$$T_0^i >_{i+1} T_1^i >_{i+1} T_2^i >_{i+1} \cdots$$

These trees are all i-minimal. We must construct a similar sequence which is $i + 1$-minimal. This is done by using the sequence of $i + 1$-subtrees as in the usual construction. But observe now that because of the gap-condition we do not create any new j-subtrees for $j \leq i$ — and hence the i-minimality is preserved under the construction.

Now to the argument for how to proceed at limit ordinals. We use the following fact about the construction

- in the first place where the bad sequence at a line and the bad sequence at the line below differ, the one tree is a subtree of the other

We then show that if we look at the columns the trees there change only finite many times. For assume not. Call a column where we have infinitely many changes for critical. Then look at the leftmost critical column. From a certain line off no trees in the columns to the left of it are changing. This means that then in all changes in the column the change is only going from a tree to a subtree. But this cannot be done infinitely many times. So there are no critical columns. In each column there are only finite number of changes and we simply define the limit tree in the column to the tree which are not changing.

As in the case for finite trees we get to line ∞

$$T_0^\infty \quad >_\infty \quad T_1^\infty \quad >_\infty \quad T_2^\infty \quad >_\infty \quad T_3^\infty \quad >_\infty \quad T_4^\infty \quad >_\infty \quad \ldots$$

by just taking the next line after taking one line for each label. The trees are j-minimal for each j.

We get a contradiction as for the simple case above. If we have an infinite $<_\infty$-descending sequence, then we get an i and an infinite $<_i$-descending sequence of immediate i-subtrees contradicting the i-minimality.

This concludes our development here — we have shown that the finite labeled trees are well ordered. There are a number of ways to continue

- connect the order types of finite labeled trees with known ordinals

- use the finite labeled trees in an analysis of iterated inductive definitions

- analyze the proof of the well ordering theorem

But — this saga continues elsewhere.